Building a Backyard Bird Habitat

Building a Backyard Bird Habitat

Scott Shalaway

STACKPOLE
BOOKS

Published by
STACKPOLE BOOKS
5067 Ritter Road
Mechanicsburg, PA 17055
www.stackpolebooks.com

Printed in the United States of America

Cover design by Caroline M. Stover
Cover photograph of American Goldfinch by Daybreak Imagery
Cover photograph of native wildflower garden by Gay Bumgarner Photography
Interior photographs by Maslowski Wildlife Productions
Illustrations by Matthew Barrick

10 9 8 7 6 5 4 3 2 1

First edition

Library of Congress Cataloging-in-Publication Data

Shalaway, Scott.
    Building a backyard bird habitat / Scott Shalaway.—1st ed.
        p. cm.
    ISBN 0-8117-2698-3 (alk.)
    1. Bird attracting. I. Title.

QL676.5.S433 2000
639.9'78—dc21   99-056905

To friend and mentor Dr. Roland Roth

and

to the memory of Dr. Fred Baumgartner

CONTENTS

Introduction   viii

Part 1   The Impacts of Backyard Birding   1

Part 2   Food   7
   Bird Food Basics   8
   Selective Feeding   10
   How to Test Seed Preference   15
   Feeding Areas   16
   Bird Feeders   17
   How to Make Suet   21
   How to Make Suet Feeders   23
   Setting Up an Insect Feeder   25
   Identifying Common Feeder Birds   26
   Avoiding Feeder Problems   28
   Preventing Window Collisions   35

Part 3   Water   37
   Backyard Water: An Irresistible Magnet 38
   The Paradox of Winter Water   39
   How to Build a Simple Water Feature   42
   How to Build a Dust Bath   42

Part 4   Nest Boxes   45
   The "Hole" Story   46
   Choosing the Best Nest Box   51
   Hot to Build a Natural-looking Nest Box 58
   The Cost of Providing Housing for Birds 59

Part 4 Nest Boxes *continued*

Protecting Nest Boxes from Predators and Competitors   60
Understanding Predation   66
Maintaining and Monitoring Nest Boxes   69

Part 5 Habitat   **75**

All-Season Gardening for Birds   76
Raising Sunflowers and Grains for Birds   77
Wildflowers for Birds   78
Trees for Birds   79
Shrubs and Hedges for Birds   81
Attracting Birds with Succulents   81
Attracting Hummingbirds   83
Fall Gardening   88
Winter Habitat   91

Part 6 Enjoying Birds More   **95**

How to Identify Unfamiliar Birds   96
Backyard Birding by Ear   100
Keeping Records   104

Appendix A   *109*

Appendix B   *115*

INTRODUCTION

When I received my Ph.D. in wildlife ecology from Michigan State University in 1979, 1 envisioned a career as a biologist for a state or federal wildlife agency. I took a road less traveled, however, and twenty years later this book offers a glimpse of some of the lessons I've learned.

I spent five years in academia teaching general biology and wildlife courses at Oklahoma State University and eight years teaching ornithology at the University of Oklahoma Biological Station. Along the way, I became hooked on birds and birding, particularly backyard birding. It wasn't really a field back then, so I blazed my own trail. I spoke to garden clubs, Audubon groups, and other conservation organizations about how to attract backyard birds. Eventually I realized that I had to move beyond the academic world to reach the masses who hungered for information about backyard birding.

In 1985, my wife and I bought ninety-five acres of West Virginia heaven so I could practice what I preach. It is here that I have tested virtually all of the suggestions I offer on these pages.

In 1986, 1 began writing a weekly syndicated nature column for newspapers, and a few years later I added magazines to my list of credits. Today my column appears in more than twenty newspapers, from Michigan and Illinois to New York and Pennsylvania, and its circulation exceeds one million readers each week. I've also written hundreds of articles for magazines such as *Birder's World, Living Bird, Pennsylvania Wildlife, Wonderful West Virginia,* and *WildBird.*

About half of my newspaper columns and most of my magazine features have been about birds, and most of those have been about attracting backyard birds. In 1995, I wrote a twelve-part series on backyard birding for *WildBird,* and followed it up with twenty-four how-to pieces in 1996. This book is my attempt to compile the best of that information into one source. It covers not only topics I think are important, but also those that readers have asked about most frequently over the years. My goals for this book are these: 1) to help you attract more birds to your backyard and 2) to help you enjoy and appreciate backyard birds more completely.

PART I

THE IMPACTS
OF
BACKYARD
BIRDING

THE IMPACTS
OF BACKYARD BIRDING

It wasn't too many years ago that bird-watching was a joke. Remember Jane Hathaway on *The Beverly Hillbillies*? Today, however, birding is respectable, even politically correct. It is environmentally acceptable, and it has become a big business. Lots of dollars change hands in the name of birds, so what was once a joke is now a legitimate avocation.

In just twenty-five years, interest in watching and attracting birds has exploded. We feed birds, house them, offer them water, plant vegetation for them, read about them, and travel to the corners of the earth to watch them.

ECOLOGICAL IMPACTS

The ecological impact of birding on birds is overwhelmingly positive. Providing food, water, and cover for backyard birds makes their lives easier and ours more enjoyable. Of course, birds got along fine for millennia without our help, but anything that makes life easier is welcome. That's the simple reason birds flock to our offerings of food, water, and cover.

The ecological benefits of our helping hands are poorly documented, but one study stands out. Stanley Temple and Margaret Brittingham studied a banded population of Black-capped Chickadees in Wisconsin for three years. One group of chickadees had access to feeders; the other did not. They discovered that: 1) most chickadees ate less than 25 percent of their food at feeders, 2) feeder birds suddenly deprived of their supplemental foods easily shifted back to natural foods, and 3) perhaps most important, nearly twice as many chickadees with access to feeders survived the winter compared to those that depended solely on natural foods.

This differential survival was most dramatic during months when temperatures dropped below zero for more than five days. The implication is that feeding stations affect survival only during winter's harshest times, and then the impact is dramatically positive. Individuals survive that might otherwise die.

Another indicator that feeding birds affects some birds positively is the range expansion certain species have experienced over the last quarter century. Several species of southwestern hummingbirds, Mourning and Inca Doves, Red-bellied Woodpeckers, Tufted Titmice, Northern Cardinals, and House Finches have all expanded their ranges northward in recent years, thanks at least in part to backyard feeding stations. In Pittsburgh, for example, Red-bellied Woodpeckers rarely appeared on Christmas Bird Counts just twenty-five years ago. Now they are common permanent residents. And Mourning Doves no longer migrate in some places where food is available throughout the winter. Cavity-nesting birds receive equally valuable benefits from birders who enjoy building nest boxes. Eastern Bluebirds, which teetered on the brink of extinction in the 1950s and 1960s, recovered quickly when birders began erecting nest boxes along bluebird trails. Since 1977, when Larry Zeleny sounded the bluebird alarm with an article in *National Geographic,* hundreds of thousands, perhaps millions, of nest boxes have been erected all across the continent. The response of Eastern, Western, and Mountain Bluebirds has been nothing short of amazing. Their populations are now comparatively stable.

Other cavity nesters such as Tree and Violet-green Swallows, Great-crested and Ash-throated Flycatchers, chickadees, titmice, nuthatches, and wrens also readily use nest boxes and are therefore less dependent on a dwindling supply of natural cavities. East of the Mississippi River it is nearly impossible to find Purple Martins that do not rely exclusively on martin houses and/or gourds.

Even horticultural plantings affect bird populations. It is difficult to determine the value of backyard plantings, but some ornithologists attribute the Northern Mockingbird's northward expansion to the fruiting shrubs highway departments have planted along the interstates in the northern half of the United States.

So even though the ecological impact of feeding birds has been poorly studied, anecdotal evidence and a few individual studies indicate that birds respond dramatically to our efforts at backyard wildlife management. Even greater, however, may be the social and economic impacts these activities exert on humans.

ECONOMIC IMPACTS

Bird-watching has become a big business. According to a 1996 survey by the U.S. Fish and Wildlife Service, nearly 63 million Americans reported watching wildlife in their backyards. The vast majority, more than 52 million, fed wild birds. In so doing, we spent more than $2.1 billion on commercially packaged wild bird food and another $831 million on feeders, baths, and nest boxes. Add binoculars, spotting scopes, photographic equipment and supplies, books, magazine subscriptions, camping gear, and travel, and the "nonconsumptive wildlife-related recreation" economy totaled more than $29 billion in 1996.

Though even Native Americans and early settlers undoubtedly fed wild birds, feeding birds did not become a serious business until relatively recently. The business we now call backyard birding was born in 1969. That was the year Peter Kilham, creator of Droll Yankee feeders, launched his now classic A-6 tube feeder. At the time, Kilham, a designer, inventor, and world-class tinkerer, was sixty-three years old. When he died in 1992 at age eighty-eight, he had watched the continent's interest in backyard birds explode.

Even Kilham's competitors acknowledge his contribution to the field. Bob Bescherer, founder and senior design engineer of Aspects, Inc., another major feeder manufacturer, puts it this way: "The A-6 got the business super-charged." Bescherer should know. For several years his company manufactured Droll Yankee's products. In 1978 he went out on his own. Today Aspects, Inc., employs twenty-five people and features a full line of tube and window feeders and the best hummingbird feeders in the business.

The next watershed moment came in 1983, though its roots date back to 1981. That's when Jim Carpenter, a horticulturist and garden center manager, opened a small wild bird specialty shop in Indianapolis. He called it Wild Birds Unlimited.

In 1983 Carpenter began selling franchises, and by 1989, there were thirty Wild Birds Unlimited stores. Most were in the Midwest. As of August 1999, Carpenter's empire included 265 stores in forty-four states and three Canadian provinces.

The success of Wild Birds Unlimited has had a tremendous ripple effect throughout the birding industry. Other franchise operations have followed in its footsteps. George Petrides opened his first Wild Bird Center in 1985. Today he oversees ninety-five stores in thirty-two states and one Canadian province.

A third franchise, Wild Bird Marketplace, opened in 1989 and ten years later had grown to twenty-nine stores in fourteen states and one Canadian province.

In addition to the booming franchise arena, scores of independent wild bird specialty retailers have sprung up all across the continent.

No discussion of the backyard birding business would be complete without a mention of the seed business. From the farmers who grow it, to the brokers, distributors, and retailers who sell it, wild bird food is a huge business. Just how huge, though, is uncertain. Insiders say there's no way U.S. consumers buy $2.1 billion worth of seed annually, but few are willing to publicly discuss their sales figures. However, the U.S. Fish and Wildlife Service figures do not seem out of line to me. If 52 million Americans spend $2.1 billion annually for birdseed, that works out to barely $40 per year per person. If anything, the numbers sound conservative.

Despite the size of the wild bird food market, it is interesting to note that many wild bird foods are not grown for that purpose. Striped sunflower seeds are exported to Europe, where they are popular snack foods. Peanuts and almonds go to the candy and "nut butter" market. Sunflower seeds and niger are grown and pressed to make vegetable oil. The bird food industry gets what is left over—those seeds judged not good enough for human consumption. Only millet is grown primarily for the wild bird food market.

TRAVEL

So far I have limited this discussion to the impacts of backyard birding. The economics of travel-related birding, however, cannot be ignored. The 1996 Fish and Wildlife Service survey assigned a value of more than $9.4 billion to food, lodging, transportation, and other travel-related expenses. Though this is labeled as "nonconsumptive wildlife-related" travel, much, if not most of it, is focused on birds.

Paul Kerlinger, former director of the Cape May Bird Observatory and now an independent consulting ornithologist, has been studying eco-tourism as it relates to birds for years. Several years ago he and David Wiedner surveyed birders who visited the CMBO. Using very conservative techniques, they concluded that 35,000 birders spent more than $5.5 million in Cape May in 1988. Similar results would be expected from surveys of any of North America's birding hot spots: Point Pelee, Ontario; Hawk Mountain, Pennsylvania; southeastern Arizona; the Texas coast; the Rio Grande Valley; and south Florida, to name just a few.

Kerlinger and Wiedner emphasize that birders represent "a dependable, low impact, and low overhead source of revenue as long as quality habitat and good birding spots remain."

In a more recent study, Kerlinger and Wiedner examined the economics of birding on a national scale. They surveyed "active" birders—those who had participated in the National Audubon Society's 89th Christmas Bird Count. They found that active birders spent an average of $1,852 per year on their hobby. That means that 43,000 Christmas Bird Counters spent nearly $80 million on bird-related activities in 1988. Most of that (71 percent) was travel-related.

The demographics of active birders underscore the economic impact birding has generated. They are well educated (74 percent are college graduates; 38 percent have graduate degrees) and earn incomes well above the national average. Most are male (63 percent), and the average age was forty-seven. Approximately 90 percent were between twenty-one and seventy years old.

WHAT DOES ALL THIS MEAN?

It means bird-watchers have power, though at the moment it is without direction or unity. There are many small groups of birders such as the American Birding Association, National Birdfeeding Society, professional ornithologists' organizations, and magazine subscribers, but none has organized itself into a formidable group.

What's needed is a generic bird conservation organization that could appeal to birders of every ilk. Once upon a time the National Audubon Society filled that niche, but during the 1970s and 1980s it evolved into a much broader conservation organization. Recent changes in NAS leadership and editorial direction offer hope that birds will once again become the primary focus of the National Audubon Society.

A "national bird conservancy" could unite all who love birds regardless of their specific interests, call attention to the environmental problems that face wild birds, be a tremendous incentive for businesses near local birding hot spots to ensure that the areas remain attractive to birds, and be a constant reminder to the business community of the power of the birding dollar. The American Bird Conservancy (1250 24th St., NW, Suite 400, Washington, D.C. 20037; founded in 1994) might be the organization to fill this vacuum.

A casual glimpse of bird-watching and bird-watchers can be deceiving. What appears at first glance to be a lightweight hobby is in reality second only to gardening as America's favorite pastime. Our activities help birds ecologically, especially during harsh winters, and the "business of bird-watching" is a multi-billion-dollar enterprise that employs tens of thousands of workers, from farmers and retailers to manufacturers, eco-tour operators, and freelance writers. Bird-watching is more than a hobby; it is a lifestyle.

PART 2

FOOD

BIRD FOOD BASICS

When shopping for wild bird food, the variety of seeds and mixes available can be overwhelming, especially for beginners. Which foods are best? Are mixes better than straight seeds? Why do some mixes cost more than others? Is there a best food? Here are some answers.

Seed Mixes. Seed mixes sold in grocery and discount department stores are often inexpensive, but beware: They can be loaded with wheat, oats, milo, and other filler grains that most birds won't eat. Judge the quality of mixes simply by reading the ingredients label. Sunflower seed should be listed first, followed by other "good" seeds—peanuts, almonds, pecans, walnuts, safflower, and white millet.

Sunflower Seeds. Black oil sunflower seeds rank as the best single food you can offer birds. These small, thin-shelled seeds are easy to open and are rich in fat and protein. Virtually every bird that visits a backyard bird feeder eats black oil seeds.

Striped sunflower seeds are larger and have thicker shells than black oil seeds. Consequently, the only birds that can eat them are those physically able to crack open these seeds, such as cardinals, jays, finches, chickadees, titmice, and woodpeckers.

Hulled sunflower seeds, which are also called sunflower kernels or sunflower chips, are ideal for most birds because they are pure food—no waste, no litter, no germination. The extra step of removing the shells, however, increases the cost. Also, hulled sunflower seeds spoil quickly when wet.

Niger. Niger (now referred to by the seed industry as "nyjer") is a tiny, black, oil-rich seed. Finches love it, and Mourning Doves and many native sparrows clean up the spillage from the tiny seed ports of finch feeders. It is imported from Africa, Asia, or India, so it is expensive.

Canola. Canola (also called rapeseed) is another small, dark, oil-rich seed that finches eat, and you'll often find it in finch mixes.

Safflower. I use safflower as a change of pace or as an ingredient in a quality seed mix. Cardinals, doves, titmice, and House Finches like safflower seeds. Some people claim that squirrels ignore safflower. Chipmunks, however, devour it.

Millet. The many varieties of millet include white proso, red, golden, and Japanese. All are eaten by a variety of ground-feeding sparrows and waterfowl, but when given a choice, most backyard birds prefer white proso millet. Consequently, it is a major ingredient in many seed mixes. One of millet's best qualities is that its seed coat is hard enough to resist weathering, but not too hard for birds to crack. But remember, this is primarily a food for ground feeders such as native sparrows and doves.

Corn. Gamebirds such as quail, pheasants, turkeys, and ducks love whole corn. At backyard feeders, whole corn attracts jays, doves, and Red-bellied Woodpeckers. Unfortunately, it also attracts crows, pigeons, grackles, and squirrels.

Cracked corn appeals to many backyard birds, but it carries some serious disadvantages. It is dusty and makes seed mixes seem dirty. It spoils quickly when wet and attracts some undesirable birds. Pigeons, starlings, House Sparrows, cowbirds, and grackles quickly find feeders filled with cracked corn, so use it sparingly if these birds are a problem. Finely cracked corn, often called chick corn or chick chops at feed mills, is often sold as an inexpensive finch food.

Milo. Milo, or sorghum, is often used as a filler seed in cheaper seed mixes. Most birds ignore it. The seed shell is just too hard for most birds to crack. Read seed mix labels and avoid blends that contain milo—unless you live in the Southwest. Sources there tell me a variety of desirable birds eat milo.

Melon Seeds. Though not commercially available at reasonable prices, melon seeds rival sunflower seeds in popularity with many birds. Begin saving and drying watermelon, cantaloupe, squash, and pumpkin seeds, and offer them as occasional treats.

Grains. Like milo, wheat and oats are cheap filler seeds that few birds prefer. Avoid mixes that include these grains.

Nut Meats. Nut meats are natural, nutritious, high-energy foods for many birds, including woodpeckers, jays, chickadees, titmice, and nuthatches. Turn autumn walks into family nut-collecting expeditions. It doesn't take long to fill a bag with acorns, hickory nuts, or walnuts. You might also find inexpensive nut meats at a local farmers' market.

Peanuts. Peanuts in the shell provide an excellent source of protein and fat for strong-billed birds such as Blue Jays, titmice, nuthatches, and some woodpeckers. Shelled peanuts attract even more birds, including White-throated Sparrows, chickadees, goldfinches, and juncos.

The key to attracting birds to backyard feeders is to offer their favorite foods. Plan your menu carefully to make your backyard buffet irresistible to the greatest variety of birds.

SELECTIVE FEEDING

The best way to attract a greater variety of birds to your feeding station is to expand the menu. Rather than just filling an ordinary hopper feeder with a generic bird food mix, think selectively. By offering specific birds and groups of birds their favorite foods, you can lure an amazing variety of birds to specific areas of the backyard.

As you spend more and more time feeding the birds, certain species will become your favorites. Many backyard birders love cardinals. Others prefer colorful finches. Still others favor woodpeckers. I'm partial to chickadees and nuthatches. You can offer specific foods that attract particular birds.

The key to feeding birds is understanding who eats what. Most birds have specific preferences that, once understood, can be used to attract specific birds to specific feeders. This applies to warblers, vireos, tanagers, orioles, thrushes, and waxwings, as well as to the more familiar seed-eating species. The "selective feeding" concept is perfect for anyone ready to step beyond a single, all-purpose mix.

To make your feeding station more selective, match birds and their foods to particular feeders. A tray, for example, is totally nonexclusive—any bird can use it. The design of some feeders, however, makes them difficult, if not impossible, for some birds to use. Hanging, bowl-style feeders such as Droll Yankee's Big Top exclude many large birds because they lack perches and appeal only to strong-footed clinging birds such as chickadees, nuthatches, and woodpeckers.

When I put up my first bird feeder in 1978, I kept it simple—sunflower seeds on a tray. Today I keep more than thirty feeders filled all around the house. Some are open to all, but most, by virtue of design and/or food, attract specific birds. I cannot tell you if the birds appreciate the selective feeders, but I certainly do. Matching birds to foods and feeders is a never-ending challenge and source of satisfaction.

SEEDEATERS

Northern Cardinals. Northern Cardinals are probably one of the most recognized birds in North America and one of the easiest to attract to backyard feeders. Even beginning birders notice that cardinals usually go for sunflower seeds in any mix. Taking advantage of this preference, a cardinal mix might include several types of sunflower seed, safflower (another favorite), and perhaps just a dash of white millet.

Cardinal food is best offered on an open tray or hopper feeder. On a cold winter day there is no more magnificent sight than a half-dozen male cardinals on a feeder. Because trays and hoppers are nonexclusive, a variety of other birds will also flock to this mix. Grosbeaks and jays are among the similar-sized birds that share the cardinal's food and feeder preferences.

Social Climbers. Second only to cardinals in popularity is a group of birds I affectionately call the "social climbers." Chickadees, titmice, and nuthatches often interact during the winter months, and they spend most of their time in trees, hence the nickname. Often a pair of Downy Woodpeckers and an occasional Brown Creeper join the group.

Like most seedeaters, the social climbers love sunflower seeds. They like nuts even more. To make any feeder irresistible to these birds, try a mixture of sunflower kernels, peanut pieces, and any nut meats that might be available. I've found that almonds, pecans, and walnuts are among their favorite nuts. Some woodpeckers, notably Red-bellied, Red-headed, Lewis', and Gila, eat corn kernels, so consider this ingredient if these woodpeckers are present.

Such a "nutty" mix will also attract squirrels and a variety of other birds, so it is especially important to match a selective feeder with this mix. A perchless feeder takes advantage of these birds' clinging ability. Droll Yankee's Big Top, Audubon Plastic's Cling-a-Wing and Super Ball, and the Duncraft Satellite satisfy this requirement. Another option is a tube feeder enclosed in a wire mesh cage. Or use chicken wire to build your own excluder cage.

Squirrels can be dealt with in several ways. Place a baffle above the feeder. Hang the feeder at least 5 feet above the ground. Bait squirrels to a far corner of the yard with relatively inexpensive whole corn kernels. Or use one of the new battery-powered antisquirrel feeders that discourage squirrels in a variety of ways.

Another selective food that appeals to the social climbers is suet. Make your own and mix with peanut butter, peanuts, other nuts, and sunflower kernels for a blend that the social climbers will eat by the billful. Suet also attracts raccoons. The best defense against raccoons is to simply take down the suet each night and store it indoors. Otherwise, you will inevitably learn how destructive raccoons can be.

Finches. Finches are among the easiest birds to attract to feeders. No matter where you live, American or Lesser Goldfinches, Common Redpolls, or House, Cassin's, or Purple Finches will almost certainly visit your feeders.

Finches like sunflower seeds and are quite content with tubes filled with black oil seeds, but niger (often, though incorrectly, called thistle) is their favorite food. These tiny, black, oily seeds are best dispensed in special finch tubes, which have tiny seed ports that prevent the seeds from spilling onto the ground and require the finches to pull out the seeds one at a time. Because there are more than 100,000 niger seeds per pound, niger tubes empty more slowly than tubes filled with sunflower seeds.

Niger, however, has one major drawback—price. Niger is expensive, and when supplies are tight, it can be downright outrageous. For that reason, many birders search for cheaper ingredients. Start with two pounds of niger, and add one pound each of finely chopped sunflower kernels and small golden millet or canola for a mix that finches in my backyard seem to enjoy as much as straight niger. Another ingredient worth trying is finely cracked corn. When I lived in Oklahoma, many people told me they used it exclusively in finch tubes and considered it a great low-end alternative to niger.

Ground Feeders. Native sparrows, juncos, towhees, and doves are just a few of the often ignored native ground feeders that visit backyard feeding stations. Perhaps they are overlooked because they are too drab. Perhaps it is because they prefer to feed on the ground rather than on feeders. Perhaps it is because they can be difficult to identify. Whatever the reason, birders who overlook native sparrows and other ground feeders miss a fascinating part of backyard feeding.

The best part about feeding these ground feeders is that their favorite foods are relatively inexpensive. Most prefer white millet and cracked corn; black oil sunflower seeds and red millet are eaten as well. The challenge with a mix for native sparrows and other ground feeders is keeping unwanted birds away. Crows, pigeons, grackles, and starlings also like these foods. The most effective solution is to build a wire mesh exclosure that sits directly on the ground or on a low tray feeder. If the mesh size is no larger than 1 1/2 inches, larger birds are excluded, but the smaller native sparrows can come and go freely. The cage also offers feeding birds a bit of protection from hawks and cats.

Gamebirds. Another group of ground-feeding birds warrants special mention. Gamebirds such as ducks, turkeys, grouse, quail, and pheasants often venture into backyards when suitable habitat is nearby. Inexpensive grains, which smaller seed-eating songbirds usually ignore and which I rarely otherwise recommend, make ideal ingredients for a gamebird mix. Whole corn kernels, millets, milo, wheat, and oats are fine for these birds.

A gamebird mix is best cast upon the ground, but then it will be eaten by a variety of rodents and other mammals as well as by the target birds. The ideal feeder for a gamebird mix is a large-capacity automatic feeder suspended from a tree. A battery-powered timer and motor dispense the food at intervals you select. For example, you might fill the feeder every three or four days and have the food automatically broadcast every morning and afternoon. When fresh snow covers the morning meal or rain spoils it, you can rest easy knowing that a fresh afternoon meal will be broadcast automatically.

OTHER FOODS

Not all birds eat seeds, so let's shift focus to other foods. What follows are a few tips for attracting species that typically eat foods other than seeds. Bluebirds and robins are good examples. Both eat insects and other invertebrates during warm weather and fruits and berries during the fall and winter. Use that knowledge to build a selective feeding program for these and other similar birds. Warblers and vireos eat mostly insects, and waxwings, tanagers, orioles, mockingbirds, catbirds, and thrashers love fruits.

Insect Eaters. Feeding insectivorous birds is simple but a bit more expensive than feeding seedeaters. Mealworms, waxworms, and maggots (all larval insects) are widely available at pet stores or most inexpensively from a variety of mail-order sources, such as Grubco, Box 15001, Hamilton, OH 45015, (800) 222-3563. Virtually all backyard birds love these live treats, especially during cold weather, when most insects are dormant. I have found that even my finest seed mixes go untouched by the seedeaters until a handful of live food is eaten.

Simply place a small custard dish or dessert bowl, or the lid of a Mason jar, on a larger tray feeder or near a perch that the birds you want to feed use. The results will be immediate and impressive. Live food is particularly effective during spring and fall migration. The list of warblers, vireos, tanagers, thrushes, and mimids that have eaten live food at my feeders is too long to mention here.

During the nesting season, especially during cool, wet weather, when insects might be hard to find, place a handful of live food in a cup near active nest boxes for parent cavity nesters to feed their young. Once again the results will amaze you.

Fruit Eaters. Fruit-eating birds, such as bluebirds and robins, can be coaxed to feeding trays with a variety of fruits. Grapes, raisins, currants, and dried cranberries are among the best baits. Sliced oranges and grapefruits attract orioles, mockingbirds, thrashers, and Red-bellied Woodpeckers. Tanagers and warblers can be tempted by bananas. And try grape jelly to attract orioles, catbirds, and wrens.

Nectar Sippers. Nectar sippers are another group that is easily attracted to backyard feeders. Hummingbirds and orioles prefer a solution of one part table sugar mixed with four parts water. Nectar feeders should be cleaned every two or three days, and fresh nectar should be added after each cleaning. To prolong the life of nectar, hang nectar feeders in shady areas protected from intense midday heat.

Though nectar is easily made with table sugar, many commercial mixes are on the market. If you prefer the convenience of premeasured or even premixed nectar, fine. I must, however, warn you of a product I've seen at a large discount department store. It was a $2.99 half-gallon jug of "hummingbird nectar." The labels reads, "Closely resembles the nectar of flowers *when mixed with sugar.*" (The italics are mine.) Three bucks for a half gallon of water, red dye, three different preservatives, and some vitamins. Hummingbirds get energy, not nutrition, from nectar. They get their nutrition from the soft-bodied invertebrates that make up a large part of their diet. Buyer, beware!

A simple source of these soft-bodied invertebrates for hummingbirds is rotten fruit. Place a few pieces of ripe fruit on a tray, and in just a few hours you will see a myriad of fruit flies. Add a piece of banana every few days, and you will have a reliable supply of live food for hummers.

Grit and Eggshells. Many birds also eat grit and eggshells. Because they lack teeth, they rely on a muscular gizzard to physically grind up their food. By eating small pebbles and grit, they add an abrasive element to the gizzard that helps digest what they eat. During most of the year, grit is readily available, but in winter, when snow covers the ground, it may be hard to find. A scoop or two of sand on a tray every couple weeks is all that is needed.

Eggshells provide calcium, which is especially important to females. During the nesting season, females mobilize calcium from their bones to build the shells that protect the eggs they lay. Crushed eggshells on a tray provide females with an easy way to repay their metabolic calcium debt. Prepare eggshells and eliminate the risk of salmonella poisoning by drying at 200° in an oven for an hour.

Roadrunners. If you live in the Southwest, you have the opportunity to operate the ultimate selective feeder, a feeder for a single species: the Greater Roadrunner. This large member of the cuckoo family adapts well to suburbia and often visits backyards, where it eats everything from snakes and lizards to small birds and eggs. Reduce the risk of predation to other backyard birds by feeding roadrunners hamburgers, hot dogs, table scraps, and canned dog or cat food.

MAKING YOUR OWN MIXES

If selective feeding sounds intriguing, you have two choices: make your own or buy prepackaged commercial mixes. By making your own formulas, you control the recipes and can tinker with them until you find the one your birds prefer best. It requires buying quantities of a variety of materials and keeping detailed records so you remember each recipe's ingredients and the time and space you need to prepare the mixes. If any of these requirements poses a problem, shop around. Several seed manufacturers and wild bird specialty stores market selective food mixes.

HOW TO TEST SEED PREFERENCE

Sometimes the best seed mixes are those you blend yourself. Why not let your backyard birds tell you what seeds they like best? Here's how to test the seed preferences of birds that visit your feeders.

Test only specific seeds, not mixes, against each other. Stock up on the basic ingredients—various sunflower seeds, niger, nuts, safflower, different millets, and cracked corn. Simplify the tests by comparing just two kinds of seed at a time. Place two identical dishes (shallow ashtrays work well) on a platform feeder outside a window. After allowing the birds to feed from the test dishes for about a week, remove all other feeders from the yard to encourage hungry birds to use the test dishes. Position the dishes side by side, and fill each with a different food. For example, one might contain black oil sunflower seed and the other white millet.

Make up a data sheet, including the date, time of day, weather, and three columns. In the left column list the birds that visit the feeders. Label the remaining two columns with the two types of food. Give the birds five minutes to resume their normal behavior, then set a timer to five minutes, and begin the first test. While the timer ticks, record the number of visits to each food. Define a visit as a bird going to one of the dishes and taking at least one piece of food. Whether a bird takes one morsel of food at a time or ten pieces, count it as a single visit. A bird must leave the dish and return to get credit for another visit. To record a visit, simply make a mark under the appropriate food for the particular bird.

When the timer sounds after five minutes, the test ends. Now go out to the testing station and switch the positions of the food trays, and repeat the test. In this way, each food will have been in both locations, thus eliminating any preference birds might have for the location of the food on the platform rather than for the food itself.

After two repetitions of the experiment, with each food in each position on the platform, one test has been completed. Repeat each test three or four times to collect enough data to make the results meaningful.

You'll also discover that various external factors such as time of day and time of year can affect the results of food preference tests. Limit your tests to three-hour blocks of time in the morning or afternoon to minimize the effect of time of day. Do most of your testing during the middle two weeks of each month so you can compare results from month to month.

After completing several tests, crunch the numbers. We will leave sophisticated statistical analyses to professional biologists. Instead, simply calculate the average number of visits to each food type (total number of visits divided by the number of reps). For example, if during three complete tests (six reps), the birds made seventy-two visits to black oil sunflower seed (average number of visits = twelve), thirty visits to white millet (average = five), you might reasonably conclude that birds prefer black oil sunflower to while millet.

To determine the preferences of an individual species, simply limit your calculations to the number of visits by that species. This is easy to do for birds such as chickadees and finches, which visit feeders often, but less frequent visitors such as woodpeckers can require many hours or even days of testing to get meaningful numbers.

Use the results of your tests to customize a seed mix that reflects the preferences of the birds in your own backyard.

FEEDING AREAS

After birds start enjoying the food you put out for them, you'll notice that different kinds of birds prefer to eat in different places. Mourning doves, towhees, and many native sparrows forage on the ground. They don't need a special feeder. Simply toss birdseed on the ground, and they'll do just fine. Actually, almost all birds, even woodpeckers, will feed on the ground if that's the only place there is food. Using feeders is more of a convenience for birdwatchers than for birds. Feeders attract birds to specific locations that are easy to see from the breakfast table, desk, or easy chair.

Give ground feeders a place to escape from cats and hawks by placing a small pile of brush a few feet from the seed. Better yet, after the holidays, lay a used Christmas tree nearby. Evergreen cuttings also provide excellent shelter from light rain, snow, and wind.

Many ground-feeding birds also use an open table feeder. A post anchored in the ground with a 24-by-24-inch board fastened to the top makes a simple but effective feeder. Larger birds such as jays, cardinals, doves, and grosbeaks will use a platform regularly. So will chickadees, titmice, and many sparrows. Place the tray at window level; the open tray makes birds easy to see or photograph. Keep seed from blowing to the ground by tacking a $1/2$-inch lip around the edge of the platform.

Hanging feeders are particularly effective when snow covers the ground. They come in a variety of styles, from the traditional wooden hopper type to high-tech, clear plastic tubes. Transparent plastic tubes are practical because they let you see when the feeder is empty. And when suspended under a plastic dome, they're difficult for squirrels to reach. Most tubes come with perches too small for larger birds. This means that finches, chickadees, and titmice can dine in relative peace. Attach a tray to the tube to permit larger birds access to the feeder.

Ball and bowl feeders are fun to watch because only small, acrobatic birds can hang on almost upside down while picking out seeds. Some woodpeckers, nuthatches, chickadees, and titmice fall into this category, and it doesn't take long for goldfinches to get the hang of it.

Another feeding area caters to suet lovers, such as woodpeckers, chickadees, and nuthatches. In fact, suet may be the best way to attract woodpeckers to your feeders. Used plastic mesh onion or orange bags make easy suet feeders, but occasionally a bird gets a foot caught in the mesh. Better, and relatively inexpensive, suet feeders are plastic-coated wire mesh suet baskets.

BIRD FEEDERS

HOW TO BUILD A TUBE FEEDER

In 1969 Peter Kilham, founder of Droll Yankee feeders, launched the modern era of backyard bird feeding by introducing his classic A-6 tube feeder. Since then, many other companies have marketed tube feeders, but only recently have I discovered a reasonable biological explanation for their success.

John Gardner, president of Wild Bird Marketplace, compares a tube feeder to a seed-bearing tree. "The tube represents the tree trunk, the perches are branches, and the food port represents a seed pod," he explained. "That's why tube feeders should be filled with sunflower seeds or some other single seed, rather than a mix." At such a food patch, birds expect to find only one type of food.

Do-it-yourselfers can capitalize on Gardner's ornitho-"logical" approach to tube feeders. You will need a length of 3- or 4-inch PVC pipe, two end caps, a 24-inch length of copper wire, a $^3/_8$-inch dowel rod, a power drill, a hacksaw, and some PVC glue.

With the hacksaw, cut a 12- to 24-inch length of PVC pipe, depending on the size of tube you prefer. Glue an end cap to one end, and drill six $^1/_8$-inch drain holes through this bottom end cap. Place the other end cap on the top of the tube, then drill two small holes through the PVC tube just below the tip of this removable end cap. These holes will anchor the copper wire hanger. The unglued top end cap can be removed to fill the feeder.

Now drill a $^3/_8$-inch hole completely through the PVC as close to the bottom as possible. Push a length of dowel rod through the holes to serve as a perch. If the feeder is intended for small birds such as finches and chickadees, the exposed perch should extend only 1 inch beyond the tube. If you want larger birds to use the feeder, each perch should be at least $1^1/_2$ inches long.

The final step is to open the seed ports. Drill a $^1/_2$-inch hole 1 inch above each perch. The bottom of the seed port should be 1 inch above the perch. You now have a PVC tube feeder with two perches. If you want more perches, space them vertically about 4 inches apart, and offset them so one perch is not directly above another. Otherwise, dinner could get messy.

To build a finch feeder, drill $^1/_8$-inch holes for the seed ports. Otherwise the directions are identical. The smaller port size will prevent tiny niger seeds and sunflower chips from pouring onto the ground.

If you are inundated with House Finches, modify the design by placing the perches an inch *above* the ports. Goldfinches and siskins are quite acrobatic and readily hang upside down to feed. House Finches are much less willing to do this. In fact, I have never seen a House Finch on one of my "House Finch–proof" tubes.

After gathering the materials and tools, building a tube feeder is a simple job. It should take less than an hour, and you will have a homemade tube that will last for many years.

HOW TO BUILD PLATFORM AND HOPPER FEEDERS

If you'd like a simple and inexpensive bird feeder, consider building your own platform or hopper feeder. These feeders attract a wide variety of birds because they are totally nonexclusive. All birds, large and small, have access to food. Occasionally jays, grosbeaks, and doves may monopolize these feeders, but usually, especially during severe winter weather, birds flock to platforms and trays.

Platform feeders can be as large or small as you care to make them, and they can be designed to be set on the ground or an old tree stump or mounted on a post or deck railing.

A basic platform feeder is simply a 12-by-18-inch piece of $^3/_4$-inch exterior plywood. Nail 1-by-3-inch furring strips around the perimeter of the feeder to prevent wind from blowing seed off the tray. Leave a 3-inch gap at one end to make cleaning easier, and drill a few $^1/_4$-inch drain holes along the platform. That's all there is to it. For ground use, attach 6-inch legs to each corner to keep the platform off wet vegetation and soil.

The major problem with platform feeders is that the food is totally exposed to the elements. A simple solution is to add four 8- to 10-inch-high corner posts, and then add a pitched roof to protect both birds and food from snow and rain.

In an attempt to provide my cardinals, towhees, and native sparrows with a more protected feeding area, I stumbled upon a simple, low-cost, multilevel platform feeder. I placed a 3-by-5-foot piece of exterior plywood on top of two sawhorses. Then I set two concrete blocks on top of the plywood and covered them with a smaller piece of plywood. I anchored the whole arrangement with another concrete block. This setup created a large, three-tiered platform feeder for cardinals, jays, sparrows, juncos, finches, and doves. The ground is reasonably protected by the large tabletop, and at first birds congregated there. But the middle level is protected by a roof that is only as high as the concrete blocks; within a few days, birds realized they could escape falling and blowing snow here, and this level became a favorite. Between snow squalls, the top board serves as an ordinary platform feeder.

Another problem with platform feeders is that they hold a limited amount of seed and must be refilled daily. The solution to this problem is a hopper feeder. Called self-feeders by some, hopper feeders are really just platform feeders modified by the addition of a seed storage bin. This reservoir holds enough seed to last at least a few days. Like platforms, hopper feeders can be as large as you care to make them. These feeders also protect the seed from rain and snow. A gabled roof, hinged on one side, makes the hopper easy to fill, and the Plexiglas sides allow easy monitoring of the food level. One word of warning: The Plexiglas sides on a hopper feeder should rest no more than $1/2$ inch above the floor. Otherwise, small birds might enter and get trapped in empty feeders.

THE ULTIMATE BIRD-FEEDING STATION

Though I keep several feeders filled with sunflower seeds and peanuts all year long, I hang the rest of my feeders in September, with thirty to forty feeders scattered all around the yard during the fall, winter, and spring. The bounty of seeds and suet attracts scores of birds, but it takes a lot of time to keep all those feeders clean and filled. So I decided to make the ultimate backyard feeding station. Here's how to do it.

The materials needed are two treated 10-foot 4x4s, one treated 12-foot 4x4, two treated 12-foot 2x4s, one piece of 2-by-6-foot $1/2$-inch exterior plywood, two 48-inch lengths of 8-inch galvanized stovepipe, a box of 3-inch galvanized screws, six 6-inch lag bolts, and at least a dozen screw-in hooks.

After gathering the materials, dig two post holes 30 inches deep and 6 feet apart. Fill the holes with about 2 inches of gravel for drainage. Then drop the 10-foot 4x4s into the holes, and backfill. Be sure the posts are level and plumb.

Next, place the 12-foot 4x4 on top of the two uprights, making sure an equal length protrudes on each end. Mark the uprights on the crosspiece, and cut out a $3/4$-inch notch on the crosspiece so it will fit snugly on the uprights. Then fasten the crosspiece to the uprights with 6-inch lag bolts. Attach a hook on each end of the crosspiece, and evenly space three more hooks along the center section of the crosspiece. You've now got a structure that resembles the mathematical symbol *pi* (π).

Now cut the two 12-foot 2x4s in half. Attach two of these 6-foot pieces perpendicular to the crosspiece, directly above the uprights. Fasten hooks on each end of these shorter crosspieces.

Then attach the two remaining 6-foot 2x4s to the uprights about 4 feet above ground level. Attach the piece of plywood to these 2x4s. Finally, slip the stovepipe on the uprights beneath the plywood. (If you use a solid piece of stovepipe, slip these pieces into place immediately after backfilling the post holes and before attaching the top crosspiece.)

You now have a permanent feeding station that will accommodate at least nine hanging feeders, and the plywood table serves as a large tray feeder for all birds and protects the ground below from rain and snow. Suet baskets can be attached directly to the uprights. The stovepipe will minimize, if not eliminate, raccoon problems. To squeeze more feeders onto the structure, space the hooks a bit more closely, enlarge the entire setup, or add some heavy-duty metal bracket hangers to the uprights.

The advantage to one large feeding station is that there's no need to trudge all over the yard to fill feeders during foul weather. And you can place the station close to a window (about 12 feet is good) so you can watch and photograph birds all day long.

If this ultimate feeding station sounds like a good idea but too much work, there are alternatives. Manufacturers such as Erva Tool & Die, Green Esteem, and the Hookery make a variety of step-in hooks, poles, and hangers that can be placed anywhere in the backyard. Use such hardware to create your own unique feeding station.

HOW TO MAKE SUET

Suet is animal fat. The best suet for feeding birds is the fat found around beef kidneys and loins; it's pure and melts smoothly. Any fat will do, however. Fat is a high-calorie, energy-rich food eaten by many birds—more than eighty species in North America. The energy birds get from suet enables them to survive from one cold winter day to the next. And many birders quickly discover that suet is a fine all-season food.

Though commercially prepared suet products are widely available, homemade suet cakes are inexpensive and easy to make. Another big plus is that you control the ingredients. Many grocery stores and butcher shops sell suet to regular customers for just pennies per pound. Some even give it away. You can also trim fat from the cuts of meat you buy. Bag this and store it in the freezer until you have several pounds. You then can either offer the birds raw suet or prepare your own cakes.

Eating raw suet is similar to eating fat from a carcass in the woods. Observations of this behavior are no doubt the root of the idea to offer suet to birds in the first place. Simply place raw suet in a suet basket or a plastic mesh bag that held oranges or onions.

The downside of raw suet is that it spoils quickly in hot weather. Birds may still eat it, but rancid suet makes a backyard feeding station messy and unpleasant. Perhaps this is why many people associate suet with cold weather and only offer it then. Certainly that's when it's most useful to birds. Easy access to high-energy food is important when days grow short and temperatures dip.

Properly prepared, however, suet is a fine all-season food. Many birds eat it all year long. Just as with seeds, however, demand is lower during summer because so much natural food abounds. And in midsummer, suet melts quickly and can soil hungry birds' feathers. So use it sparingly in July and August.

If you opt to make your own suet cakes, cut the suet into small pieces or run it through a meat grinder. Then place it in a pan or a double boiler and melt over low heat. This is called rendering.

To make the suet more appealing to a greater variety of birds, add portions of cornmeal, oatmeal, sunflower seeds, peanuts, almonds, walnuts, bacon grease, peanut butter, and/or shortening. Raisins, currants, or chopped fruits sometimes attract bluebirds, robins, mockingbirds, catbirds, and orioles.

Here's one recipe that works well: Melt 1 cup of lard and 1 cup of chunky peanut butter, combine, then stir in 2 cups of quick-cook oats, 2 cups of cornmeal, 1 cup of white flour, and $1/3$ cup of sugar. This recipe came from Martha Sargent of Trussville, Alabama. Pour into square freezer containers about $1^1/2$ inches thick. Allow to cool, then cut into cakes and store in the freezer. Experiment to find the recipe that works best in your yard.

Vegetable shortening also makes a fine suet substitute. Burt Princen, a friend who lives in Peoria, Illinois, has been feeding birds shortening for nearly thirty years. He simply smears a few spoonfuls on the trunk of a tree outside his patio window. He buys whatever shortening is on sale in three-pound cans, and all the suet-eaters love it.

HOW TO MAKE SUET FEEDERS

Woodpeckers, chickadees, titmice, nuthatches, and Brown Creepers are among the most entertaining and popular visitors to backyard feeders. Suet is often the key to attracting and holding these acrobatic birds. Build a suet feeder, and they will come—and so might kinglets, wrens, and maybe even a few wintering warblers in southern latitudes.

SUET CONES

A favorite with kids and parents, pine cones dipped in melted suet are the essence of simplicity. Collect a few pine cones, preferably mature open cones, and melt some suet in a pan over low heat. Make the recipe even more appealing by adding a bit of peanut butter. When the suet liquefies, dip the pine cones in the suet. Then sprinkle some sunflower seeds on the congealing suet. Suspend the suet cone from a tree branch or metal hook, and you're in the suet business.

SUET BAGS

For no-cost suet feeders, recycle plastic mesh onion and orange bags as suet bags rather than tossing them in the trash. Simply place a suet cake or a hunk of raw suet inside the bag, and hang it near other feeders. Check the suet bag several times each day. It is conceivable, though unlikely, that a bird might gets its feet tangled in the mesh. Be vigilant and observe the backyard birder's first commandment: do not harm; the welfare of the birds comes first.

SUET LOGS

Any small log can be converted into a suet feeder. Find one with a knothole or two, and it's ready to go. Just smear the hole full of suet. If you can't find a knotty log, nail bottle caps up and down the length of a foot-long log, and smear suet into the bottle caps. Alternatively, you can drill a series of $1^{1}/_{2}$-inch holes about $^{3}/_{4}$ inch deep, and fill these holes with suet. Insert a screw eye on one end of the log, and hang it from a tree. All suet eaters have strong, clinging feet, so perches are unnecessary.

SUET BASKETS

Suet baskets are a bit more difficult to make because they require working with some form of wire mesh, which can be troublesome to cut. You will need a 6-by-14-inch piece of $^1/2$-inch wire mesh and three pieces of wood that measure 2 by 6 by $^3/4$ inch thick.

Bend the mesh into a U shape with 6-inch sides and a 2-inch base. Staple two of the wooden pieces on the open ends of the U. The basket is now complete. Screw one end of the final piece of wood to one of the wooden uprights so that it swivels back and forth to allow you to put suet into the basket. Secure the other end with a hook and screw eye. Finally, place a screw eye into the top, and hang the feeder.

WOODPECKER TREES

During a visit to the A. B. Brooks Nature Center in Wheeling, West Virginia, I saw something I had never seen before: a pileated woodpecker repeatedly coming to a suet feeder. Pileateds are magnificent crow-size woodpeckers that live in mature forests.

Jeff Donahue, the naturalist at the nature center, told me three pileateds regularly visited their "woodpecker tree," a special suet feeder designed especially for woodpeckers, though other suet lovers use it, too. But the birds never cooperated when I stopped by. Finally I got lucky. I was at the nature center taping a segment for a television show when the large crested woodpecker swooped into view and onto the woodpecker tree.

The woodpecker tree consists of a 4x4 post anchored in the ground. On the top half of the post, a series of inch-deep holes about 2 inches in diameter run down two sides of the post. The holes are about 12 inches apart. Only the two sides of the post visible from the nature center's viewing window are used; this prevents birds from hiding on the back side of the post.

Building a woodpecker tree is easy. Sinking it into the ground in the middle of winter is not. So I devised a simple variation. I cut a 2x4 down to 6 feet in length and used a $1^1/2$-inch wood bit to drill four $^3/4$-inch-deep holes on the top half of the 2x4. I placed the holes about a foot apart. I also drilled two pairs of $^1/8$-inch holes through the 2x4—one pair near the top, the other near the middle. Next, I cut two lengths of plastic-coated electrical wire and laced them through the $^1/8$-inch holes.

Then I took my modified woodpecker tree out to a tree I can see from my office window and strapped it to the trunk with the electrical wire. The final step was filling the holes with suet and/or peanut butter. Soft recipes can simply be smeared into the holes. Harder suet blocks must be pressed or even hammered into the holes.

Once the woodpecker tree was filled and in place, I sat back and watched. Within three hours, nuthatches, chickadees, and downy woodpeckers discovered the new feeder. It quickly became one of the busiest spots in the yard. Not bad for a feeder that cost less than $5 for materials and took less than fifteen minutes to make. When I get my first pileated, success will be complete.

SETTING UP AN INSECT FEEDER

If you'd like to attract birds throughout the spring and summer, try stocking a feeder with live insects. You'll be amazed at the variety of new birds that visit an insect feeder. Wrens, vireos, warblers, and maybe even Scarlet Tanagers will stop by and compete with woodpeckers, nuthatches, and other regular visitors. In suitable habitat, live food may even tempt bluebirds, robins, catbirds, and mockingbirds.

An insect feeder is simple to set up. The easiest way is to attract insects to existing feeders. Start with some hummingbird nectar: Mix one part table sugar and four parts boiling water, cool, and chill. Don't use honey; it can harm birds and bees. Add some stale pancake syrup and juice from canned fruit, and blend the mixture with a soft, ripe banana.

Place a small container of this sweet cocktail on a tray feeder, or paint the trunk of a tree with the sweet concoction, which simulates a natural sap flow and works just as well. Locate your insect feeder in a far corner of the yard, because the slurry will attract bees and wasps in addition to myriad other insects.

Shortly after the insects arrive, so will the birds. Virtually all nesting birds feed their chicks insects, so expect to see almost any bird at an insect feeder. Flycatchers, warblers, vireos, and other insect eaters will find it irresistible. During spring migration, the array of birds that visit will change. Even hummingbirds, when they return, will hover above the slurry and pick off gnats, flies, and other soft-bodied insects.

Another option is to use mealworms at your regular feeders. Put a small handful on a tray feeder, and cover them with a piece of bark so they don't overheat and dry out. Bait shops and pet stores sell mealworms, but they are expensive. An aptly named Ohio company, Grubco, can ship mealworms directly to your door; call (800) 222-3563 to order.

IDENTIFYING COMMON FEEDER BIRDS

If you feed birds, you probably enjoy watching them, but you may not be able to identify many of the birds you see at your feeder. You may recognize cardinals and Blue Jays, but the rest all seem to look alike. If so, you are among the majority of 63 million Americans who feed birds but cannot identify more than a few. Perhaps it seems an impossible task—field guides illustrate hundreds of species. But learning backyard birds is not nearly as difficult as it may seem, especially in winter. Fewer than twenty-five species commonly visit winter feeders, so the key isn't wading through a voluminous field guide, it's simply knowing which birds to expect.

Here's a list of some common feeder birds and thumbnail sketches of their most conspicuous characteristics. They may not all visit your feeders, and you may see others that are not on the list, but by learning this basic cast of characters, you'll be able to recognize 90 percent of the winter birds that brighten your yard. Use a field guide to review the field marks, and you'll master them all quickly.

Downy Woodpecker. Smallest woodpecker; black and white; white back and belly; bill shorter than head; males have red spot on back of head; hitch their way up tree trunks.

Hairy Woodpecker. Like Downy but larger; bill heavy and longer than head.

Red-bellied Woodpecker. Poorly named; pale pink wash on belly; white rump; zebralike black-and-white-barred back; white wing patches flash in flight; crown and nape red on male; red nape only on female.

Black-capped and Carolina Chickadees. Look-alike species; small; black cap and throat; gray body; check field guide for range maps.

Tufted Titmice. Small; crested; gray with black forehead; pale rusty sides under wings.

White-breasted Nuthatch. Black cap; white face and breast; acrobatically climbs headfirst down tree trunks; call a nasal "ank, ank."

Blue Jay. Large, bold, aggressive; crested; blue wings and tail with black bars and white patches; black "necklace" on white chest.

Northern Cardinal. Males bright red with black face; females duller; large orange bill; crested.

American Goldfinch. Small; dull, yellow-green or brownish plumage in winter; dark wings with lighter wing bars; often abundant at feeders.

House Finch. Reddish and sparrowlike; head, bib, and rump bright red; cap brown; belly white with brown streaks; females drab, streaky brown.

Purple Finch. Easily confused with House Finch, but less common; more reddish overall; belly *not* streaked; huskier than House Finch.

Pine Siskin. Small, streaky brown finch; bill thin and pointed; base of tail and wing feathers pale to bright yellow.

Evening Grosbeak. Chunky, a bit larger than a cardinal; huge cardinal-like bill; yellow forehead, eyebrow, and body; wings black with large, white patch.

Mourning Dove. Brownish gray, chunky body; small head; long, pointed tail; distinctive wing whistle as dove takes off; call a mournful, owl-like cooing.

Song Sparrow. Brown; dark stripe borders white throat; streaking on breast often converges to a prominent central spot; pumps tail in flight.

White-throated Sparrow. White throat; light eyebrow stripe turns yellow in front of eye; bill dark. Whistles high, pure "Old Sam Peabody, Peabody, Peabody" any time of year.

White-crowned Sparrow. Similar to White-throat; black-and-white-striped crown; pink bill; pale throat, but not bright white; no yellow on face.

Tree Sparrow. Rusty crown; plain gray breast with dark central spot; two white wing bars.

Eastern Towhee. Formerly called Rufous-sided Towhee; red eyes; black hood and upper body; rusty sides; white belly, wing patches, and tail corners.

Dark-eyed Junco. Common visitor at backyard feeders; often called snowbird; charcoal gray body; white belly and outer tail feathers; light-colored bill.

AVOIDING FEEDER PROBLEMS

A feeder filled with sunflower seeds will attract a variety of visitors. Unfortunately, not all of them are birds. Part of the downside of feeding wild birds is dealing with unwanted visitors. It may be gluttonous squirrels and raccoons raiding feeders day and night. It may be hawks and cats that eat the intended guests. Sometimes it is the less desirable birds that many of us would rather discourage—pigeons, grackles, House Sparrows, and starlings. Every problem, however, has a solution, or at least a way to reduce the severity of the problem.

SQUIRRELS

Before you can control squirrels, you have to understand them. They are incredibly athletic. Gray and fox squirrels can jump vertically 5 feet and horizontally 10 feet. To isolate a feeder, therefore, it must be at least 5 feet above the ground and 10 feet from the nearest tree. That sounds like a pretty barren backyard. Such a feeder might discourage squirrels, but it's likely to discourage birds, too.

There are three practical choices: remove the squirrels, battle them, or live with them. Having tried all three alternatives in various parts of the country, I have decided that coexistence is the best option.

The conclusion that coexistence is the best strategy often is a last resort. Removing them seems so easy. You buy a live trap, bait it with peanut butter, humanely trap the offenders, then transport them to a distant park. Or you hire a wildlife damage control specialist to remove the squirrels.

Unfortunately, squirrels are a lot like House Sparrows—there seems to be a never-ending supply. Each time you remove a few squirrels, others replace them. After a few weeks of this exercise in futility, you are ready for Plan B: buying a "squirrel-proof" feeder or devising makeshift devices to make existing feeders squirrel resistant. Retired engineers and do-it-yourselfers find this option particularly appealing. Surely they can outfox a squirrel.

Unfortunately, squirrels are very clever. "Squirrel-proof" feeders are often foiled in a matter of weeks, sometimes days. Clever counterweighted designs that close when used by a larger animal fall victim to pairs of squirrels that use the feeder like a seesaw to take turns eating. Among the most effective designs are those that enclose the feeder in a large mesh wire cage. Small birds come and go, but squirrels are stymied. The cage must be large enough, however, that squirrels cannot reach into the food supply.

Another strategy is to use baffles above and below the feeder. These can be effective, but because the feeder must be beyond a squirrel's vertical jumping range, it is too high to fill without a stepladder or stool, which can be dangerous.

The most recent weapon designed to discourage squirrels might be classified as chemical warfare. Sprinkle a light film of hot pepper–based powder on each bag of seed, and the squirrels will go elsewhere. At least, that's what the ads claim. Or buy pretreated seed. Theoretically, squirrels' keen senses of smell and taste render treated food unpalatable. I've tried the powder, and sure enough, my birds did not mind it at all. I found the effect on squirrels inconclusive, so I polled readers of my syndicated newspaper column. Half said the powder worked just as advertised; their squirrels hated the stuff. The other half said it had no effect; their squirrels were unbothered.

All these experiences have led me to conclude that squirrels really are not worth all this time and effort. So I developed my own strategy: If you can't beat 'em, feed 'em. I bait squirrels to a far corner of the yard with inexpensive whole corn. The squirrels are content, and my life is a lot simpler.

RACCOONS

Raccoons may not be as nimble and agile as squirrels, but they are incredibly strong and smart. If food is left in feeders overnight, raccoons will eventually find it. Because they are much longer than squirrels, they can often reach beyond a squirrel baffle for food. I once observed a particularly clever raccoon learn how to get to food that was just barely out of reach under a squirrel baffle. It could reach the top of the feeder, but not the food. After a few tries, it learned to twist the bottom part of the hanging feeding counterclockwise while clinging to the squirrel guard's support post above the feeder with its hind feet. After a few complete turns, the bowl that held the food fell to the ground, and the raccoon climbed down the tree and gorged on sunflower seeds.

Raccoons also love suet. If suet bags and baskets are not firmly anchored to a tree or post, raccoons often carry off both suet and feeders.

The simplest solution to raccoon problems is to fill your feeders every morning with just enough food so that they are empty by nightfall. If this is not possible, put the feeders in the house or garage every night. This one extra step sure beats replacing feeders every week or two.

HAWKS

The birds in my backyard are always skittish. I give them food, water, and cover, yet every time a car drives by or I step out to fill the feeders, a whoosh of wings fills the air.

Several times each year, I'm reminded why birds are so jumpy. The yard teems with birds—doves, chickadees, titmice, goldfinches, House Finches, and cardinals. Suddenly, in unison, like a single organism, they fly away. Moments later, a large shadow crosses the yard. I leave my desk and hurry to the other side of the house. There, in the apple tree that holds several feeders, sits a Sharp-shinned Hawk.

Just the appearance of the hawk drove all the yard birds into hiding. Like a gunslinger that terrorizes the town in an old western, a Sharp-shinned Hawk strikes fear in the hearts of small birds. Those unacquainted with the ways of the sharpie often end up plucked and swallowed.

Sharp-shinned Hawks eat birds. They are stealthy predators, attacking suddenly from a hidden perch or from above. That doesn't make them "bad." That's just what they do. If you feed birds, remember that. Sooner or later, a Sharp-shinned Hawk, its larger cousin, a Cooper's Hawk, or even an American Kestrel will visit your feeders. And it won't be sunflower seeds they're after.

The natural reaction to predators that kill the birds we work so hard to attract is horror and loathing. But nature's cycle of life and death is not good or bad. It's just the way it is.

Hawks enjoy federal and state protection, so the only thing you can do to protect feeder birds from aerial predators is to ensure that the backyard includes some escape cover. Feeders should be within a short flight of dense protective cover—trees and shrubs no more than 10 feet away.

CATS

Pet cats, when allowed outdoors, are backyard birds' worst nightmare. Feral cats—unwanted, abandoned house cats—are even worse. They sometimes subsist on wild birds. Often they stalk bird feeders. Nothing irks me more than to see a big old tom wander up the hill just after I find a bloody pile of yellow and black feathers under one of my feeders.

Feral cats are a significant problem. Estimates of the U.S. feral cat population range from 10 to 30 million. Their impact on songbirds must be staggering. If each kills just 10 birds per year, that's 100 to 300 million fewer birds in our backyards.

The solution to the feral cat problem lies in controlling the supply of cats. Ideally, every cat should be a house pet. When cat owners understand the damage their pets do to the natural world, most will keep their cats indoors. Those who simply cannot bring themselves to "imprison" their pets permanently can do several things.

First, neuter pet cats before they breed. Cats multiply rapidly. A single female can bear two to ten kittens three times per year when food and shelter are available. That means one unwanted female cat can produce thirty offspring by year's end, not to mention the grandchildren her daughters will bear before the year is up.

The second strategy for reducing the impact of an indoor-outdoor cat is to put a bell on its collar. Until the cat learns to walk without sounding the bell—and it will—birds will be warned when it approaches.

Third, keep feeders 6 to 10 feet from vegetation. On one hand, nearby vegetation is necessary for birds to escape hungry hawks, but if feeders are too near a dense shrub, cats will stalk feeders from that nearby cover. Cover near feeders is critical, but it must be neither too close nor too far away.

Meanwhile, landowners with an existing feral cat problem do have options. A dog in the backyard discourages cats from making your place a regular dinner spot. Some experts suggest putting out cat food for the ferals, reasoning that if the cats are well fed, they won't bother the birds. But the best solution is to eliminate feral cats. Laws vary, but even feral cats are protected by some state, county, and municipal laws. Complain loudly and repeatedly to county and city authorities about feral cats. Educate officials about the impact of cats on wild birds.

RATS

Just the thought of rats repulses many people. They live under our homes, in attics, in sewers and alleys. Wherever you find people, you're likely to find rats. They eat garbage and thrive in the urban jungle. They even live in suburban backyards, sometimes those littered with bird food.

Rats thrive because they are equally at home in a barn, a middle-class home, a tenement, or a sewer. They can climb, dig, jump, and swim, so few obstacles are effective barriers. They feast on our trash and can live in a garbage dump. And they are prolific. Females can breed the day after giving birth and often do. Just twenty-one days later, she bears a litter of seven or eight pinkies. They wean their young in three weeks, just as the next litter arrives. A healthy female can breed when twelve weeks old and may have six litters per year.

Farm supply and garden stores often recommend poison for a rat problem. I do not. Most poisons are broad spectrum and kill anything that eats it. Instead, clean up the ground under the feeders, and rake it every few days. By removing the food supply, you make your backyard much less desirable to rats. Often they move on.

A more direct approach is to set traps, which look like large mousetraps, near any rat holes under the feeders. Use peanut butter for bait, and trap only at night, when the rats are most active. Birds will go after the peanut butter during the day, and if the traps are set, you will get illegal, heartbreaking "nontarget losses."

Another technique is to flood rat burrows. Underground tunnels lead to nests where colonies of ten to twelve individuals gather. Even if the rats don't drown (they're good swimmers), a few good soakings may encourage them to go elsewhere.

These solutions work only on a small scale—in a single yard or home. An apartment house or a whole neighborhood infested with rats represents a much bigger problem. Ultimately, the solution is to make the entire area unsuitable for rats. Clean up the trash, and make garbage cans and buildings rat-proof.

UNWELCOME BIRDS

Though some people welcome all birds to their feeding station, many try to discourage certain species they consider undesirable. These include pigeons, House Sparrows, starlings, grackles, cowbirds, and crows. Larger species, such as pigeons, grackles, and crows, can be excluded by placing feeders inside wire mesh cages. These exclusion devices are even more effective against large birds than they are against squirrels.

Smaller undesirables, such as cowbirds and House Sparrows, are almost impossible to exclude. A better strategy might be to specialize in niger and suet feeders when these birds become a problem. Like rats, they often move on if they cannot find their favorite foods.

KEEPING THINGS CLEAN

A major concern, especially in suburbia where peer pressure puts a premium on a tidy yard, is the mess that accumulates under any feeder. Seed shells and bird droppings can be unsightly. Neighbors who might not yet share your enthusiasm for birds might even consider your feeding station an eyesore.

The simple solution is to clean the ground beneath the feeders regularly. Rake the hulls and droppings once or twice a week, and your yard will look great all winter long. A clean feeding station is also much healthier for the birds. A variety of avian diseases can be transmitted at soiled feeders, so there is also a biological incentive to keep your feeders clean.

Another aesthetic consideration is the uneaten seeds that germinate under feeders each spring. A crop of millet or sunflowers might be a great idea, but chances are that under the feeders is not the best location. Here again the solution is simple. Offer waste-free foods—seeds from which the shells have been removed. Peanut, pecan and walnut pieces, and hulled sunflower seeds are readily available, and many birds love them. Because these foods are free of waste and shells, there is little need to rake and no weeds in the spring. No-mess seeds are also great for feeders on decks, patios, and porches. It virtually eliminates messes that even spouses sometimes find intolerable.

KEEPING BIRDS HEALTHY

Perhaps the best reason to maintain a tidy feeding station is to ensure the health of feeder birds. Dirty feeders and yards are breeding grounds for a variety of avian diseases.

One problem is salmonellosis. Birds can die from food poisoning just like people can. A few years ago, the U.S. Fish and Wildlife Service issued a press release announcing an increase in the number of cases of avian salmonellosis showing up around backyard feeders. Cardinals, siskins, and goldfinches seem most often affected. They usually show no outward signs of illness; they just die suddenly. Often people think the birds have been poisoned, and in a sense, they have.

Avian salmonellosis is a group of diseases caused by bacteria in the genus *Salmonella*. In humans, salmonella causes food poisoning, characterized by abdominal pain and diarrhea, as well as more serious illnesses. Avian salmonella infections are natural and are just one of many factors that control wild bird populations. Occasionally, however, outbreaks occur near bird feeders, and scores of birds can die.

The infection can flare up at any time of year. It is associated with unsanitary environmental conditions, not weather. Salmonella infections can be transmitted in many ways, but die-offs at feeders are caused by fecal contamination of food. Salmonella carriers visit feeders and deposit their droppings on feeding trays and on the ground beneath feeders. Healthy birds then eat the tainted seed and become infected. Whenever a large group of birds gathers to eat in one place, some of the food may be fouled by droppings of infected birds, and the possibility of a salmonella outbreak exists.

Controlling avian salmonella outbreaks is simply a matter of keeping feeders clean and regularly raking the spilled and soiled seed that accumulates under feeders. It's a good idea to wear rubber gloves so you don't directly touch any of the soiled material. A good preventive measure is to disinfect your feeders with a household bleach after they've accumulated a lot of fecal matter. I've found that my feeders, particularly seed trays, get especially dirty in wet weather. If you find dead birds under your feeders, take the feeders down, wash and disinfect them, and stop feeding for about a week.

Another disease can flare up around feeders when people use moldy seed. Aspergillosis is caused by the fungi that makes seed moldy. The disease spreads when birds inhale the fungal spores found in moldy seed. Symptoms of aspergillosis include difficulty breathing, indicated by rapid opening and closing of the bill, wing droop, and death. Sick birds may be weak and easy to capture, but don't pick them up. Concentrate instead on correcting the problem. Throw out moldy seed, and buy fresh seed as you need it.

In the mid-1990s a new disease, which causes eye infections among House Finches, flared up over a large area in the eastern United States. The original report called the disease *conjunctivitis,* a general term for any infection of the eye membrane. This type is restricted to birds. The symptoms of avian conjunctivitis are swollen, runny, or encrusted eyes. Sometimes the eyes swell shut and the birds cannot see, making them easy prey, and most probably succumb to predators rather than to the disease itself. The first cases were reported in February 1994 in Maryland, Virginia, and New Jersey. By mid-April the National Wildlife Health Center (NWHC) in Madison, Wisconsin, was investigating. Laboratory tests identified the culprit as a bacteria called *Mycoplasma.* Fortunately, the disease seems restricted to House Finches and seems to have begun to run its course.

The NWHC makes the following suggestions to minimize the spread of any contagious diseases at feeding stations:

- Large numbers of birds in a small space helps spread disease. If your feeding station is crowded, spread the feeders out or add additional feeders.
- Clean feeders and the feeding area regularly, at least once a week. Disinfect feeders with a solution of one part bleach to nine parts water. Use smaller-capacity feeders, and empty them completely when cleaning them. Feeders with rough surfaces and cracks are difficult to sanitize

and should not be used. Move feeders around periodically to reduce the buildup of infectious organisms.

- If you see sick or dead birds at your feeders, notify your state wildlife agency or a local nature center. Immediately clean the feeders, and stop feeding for at least a month.

PREVENTING WINDOW COLLISIONS

The thud of feathered body on glass is familiar to anyone who feeds birds. Sometimes it happens several times a day. Most window collisions are not fatal, but each year an unknown number of birds die.

Dr. Daniel Klem, Jr., biology professor at Muhlenburg College in Allentown, Pennsylvania, spent twelve years studying window collisions and concluded that birds are incapable of perceiving glass as a barrier. He identified two types of windows that deceive birds. One type appears invisible and creates a see-through effect, especially if there is an open window on the other side of the room that creates the illusion of a passageway through the house. The other type is strongly reflective and mirrors outside habitat. In either case, birds cannot perceive the glass and attempt to either fly through the glass to daylight or into the vegetation reflected by the glass.

While some birds may fly into windows during normal flight, other factors contribute to most collisions. Some birds, such as accipiter hawks and Ruffed Grouse, are at risk because of their habit of flying through restricted flight lanes in dense vegetation. Accipiters chase smaller birds through wooded areas, and grouse routinely fly through dense forest understory cover. In both cases, these birds are guided by bright areas ahead that indicate open spots in the vegetation. Bright spots behind or reflected in glass create the same impression.

Most other victims are usually in some way distracted. They may be escaping danger, involved in a chase, disoriented by unusual weather or lighting, or under the influence of alcohol, as when waxwings eat fermented berries.

Window collisions may seem like a trivial problem, but more than 63 million of us feed birds in our backyards. If each records only three window kills per year (a conservative estimate), it is not unreasonable to assume that staggering numbers of birds may die at windows annually. This doesn't mean we should stop feeding birds near our houses, but Klem does offer some suggestions for reducing the frequency of window collisions.

- Move feeders and birdbaths close to windows (within a foot or two) so birds can't build up lethal momentum if they do hit the glass.
- Alter the appearance of transparent windows by covering the surface with objects less than 4 inches apart, such as strips of cardboard, paper plates, mobiles—anything that makes the window more visible. This is why hawk silhouettes sometimes work, not because they look like predators.
- Change the appearance of mirrored windows by painting with soap or covering with a fine gauze netting.
- Keep drapes closed and lights off to reduce the effect of a see-through passage behind the glass.

PROJECT FEEDERWATCH

To make your backyard birdfeeding hobby more meaningful, consider joining Project FeederWatch, an annual, nationwide survey of the status of feeder bird populations. Only a large core of volunteers can collect field data on a continental scale. Thanks to their efforts, ornithologists are gaining a much better understanding of the birds that visit backyard feeders. To participate, contact Project FeederWatch, Cornell Lab of Ornithology, 159 Sapsucker Woods Road, Ithaca, NY 14850.

PART 3

WATER

BACKYARD WATER: AN IRRESISTIBLE MAGNET

When I was a graduate student, I lacked the time and money required to manage my small backyard. As I traveled back and forth to my study site each day, though, I noticed that quite a few homes had bird feeders and baths.

One hot August morning, after a thunderstorm had relieved a month-long drought, I noticed many birds gathered in a yard at one of the houses near my study site. I stopped and watched. Over the course of thirty minutes, robins, cardinals, doves, Song Sparrows, a catbird, a House Wren, and a Downy Woodpecker visited that yard. The lure was an old concrete birdbath that had filled with water during the early-morning downpour.

As the birds came and went, I noticed a definite method to their routine. First they drank. Then they bathed. A few seemed to linger and soak. I watched one cardinal intently. It bent its legs, then dipped down and submerged its body. As it emerged, it flapped its wings to help saturate its body. Then it hopped onto the edge of the bowl, fluffed its feathers, and preened. Reaching back to the base of the tail, it massaged a small gland with its bill. The gland released a dab of oil, which the cardinal then smeared over its feathers. The oil cleans, lubricates, and waterproofs the feathers so they will last until the next time the bird molts.

Keeping feathers clean and healthy is routine maintenance; without it, birds couldn't survive. Feathers protect the skin, minimize body weight, insulate and streamline the body, enable birds to fly, and provide the colors that help birds recognize each other. A dependable supply of fresh water helps birds keep their feathers fit.

Water also helps birds meet some of their daily physiological needs. On hot days, birds sometimes seem to soak in a bowl of fresh water just to cool off. Clean drinking water also enables birds to replace the water they lose by evaporation.

The simplest way to provide water is to put up a birdbath. It could be anything from an inverted garbage can lid on a tripod of rocks to a polypropylene saucer on a metal stand or even a small pond complete with pump and waterfall. You are limited only by your imagination and budget. Regardless of how sophisticated you may choose to get, here are some tips to keep in mind:

- Keep the water no more than 2 inches deep. This is not a problem with most saucer-style baths, but if you install a small pool or pond, pile a stack of rocks to make one end shallow enough for small birds to bathe.
- Place the bath in open shade. It should be shaded between noon and 4 P.M. so the water doesn't get too hot. Overhead cover also provides safe haven when a cat or bird-eating hawk enters the area.
- Keep a bath at least 15 feet from any feeders. Seed hulls and droppings soil water rapidly.
- Change the water and rinse the bowl daily. A plastic scouring pad makes quick work of most grime. Algae, droppings, and windblown debris can turn a birdbath into a germ-infested "soup" in just a few days.
- Add a mister or a dripper. Birds find the sound of moving water irresistible. Dripper valves can regulate the flow of water from a steady stream to just a few drops per minute. Misters spray a fine mist of water above the bath, or they can be placed in a tree or shrub to simulate a refreshing summer rain. Warblers, vireos, hummingbirds, orioles, and tanagers are just some of the Neotropical migrants that enjoy bathing in a humid, tropiclike mist.

THE PARADOX OF WINTER WATER

Some things make sense and some do not. Feeding birds in winter, for example, makes sense. Natural foods are in short supply, weather can be harsh, and handouts attract birds to places where it is convenient to watch them. Furthermore, because birds are mobile and accustomed to searching for patchy food sources, research shows that they do not develop an unhealthy dependence on artificial food sources. Feeding winter birds is good for birds and birders.

Providing winter water, on the other hand, makes far less intuitive sense. Certainly birds do not bathe during freezing weather, so why tempt them? Can't they just eat snow or get water from the food they eat? And won't the water just freeze and crack the birdbath? Winter water sounds like a screwy idea.

But it's not. Like food, water is in short supply during winter. In some places, it freezes. In others, winter is dry. In any case, water is a valuable resource that attracts birds like monarchs to milkweed. So if you're a backyard birder who wants to attract more birds, make water a part of your landscape.

Because of the likelihood of freezing temperatures, though, providing winter water is not simply a matter of filling a conventional birdbath every day. Ceramic, glass, and concrete baths often crack when the water in them freezes, so even though these are among the most popular types of baths, winter requires a concession to nature. Freeze-proof materials such as metal or plastic bowls are necessary. But even that's not enough, unless you're willing to fill the bowl with warm water several times a day. An efficient winter birdbath also requires a heating element—a device to keep at least some of the water from freezing during even the coldest conditions. Electric submersible heaters, based on technology used to make livestock water heaters, work very well. Most are thermostatically controlled and kick on at about 40 degrees F. A safeguard to look for is a built-in control that shuts the heater off if the bath runs out of water or if the bath gets tipped over. Also, be sure to use a heavy-duty, outdoor-rated extension cord.

Environmentally minded birders might prefer a solar-powered drinking device. The Solar Sipper, manufactured by the Happy Bird Corp., uses passive solar energy to keep water liquid down to 20 degrees F. And it is designed strictly as a drinking device so birds can't accidentally immerse themselves on cold days.

If cost is a factor in your decision to add winter water, start with an old garbage can lid and fill it with hot water every morning. It won't take the birds long to learn that water is available for only a few hours each day. After you're convinced that birds enjoy winter water, it will be easier to justify the $70 to $100 that a bath and heater cost.

One important word of caution must be added here: Under no circumstances use chemicals of any sort to prevent birdbath water from freezing. To do so risks poisoning your birds with toxic materials.

Birds use water all year long. It is one of the requisites of life. Without it, they would die. When standing water is available, birds drink it. They sometimes eat snow, too, but ingesting ice crystals in winter is counterproductive to the seasonal feeding frenzy designed to fuel their metabolic fires.

Yet birds survived freezing winters quite well for eons before anyone ever thought of providing them with heated water. Birds adapted to subfreezing winters can extract water metabolically from the solid foods they eat, even from seemingly dry seeds. That's because these seeds contain as much as 10 percent water, even though they appear to be completely dry.

But winter birdbaths make life a whole lot easier for birds, especially in northern climes. When streams, ponds, and puddles freeze over, heated birdbaths ensure a reliable—and often the only—water supply. Though apparently not physiologically necessary, birds seem to prefer to drink when possible. Perhaps drinking free water is energetically cheaper than extracting it metabolically from dry food. Whatever the explanation, birds drink water all year long when it's available.

During subfreezing weather, birds seem to know not to bathe. They perch on the rim of the saucer or sometimes on the heating element to avoid getting their feathers wet while drinking. They lose little heat through their naked, scaly feet, because minimal blood flows through the lower extremities. And thanks to a countercurrent arrangement of venous and arterial blood flow in the feet, heat loss is low. Cooler venous blood returning to the heart is warmed by surrounding vessels of warmer arterial blood.

In more southern areas, where freezing temperatures are less common, birds will drink *and* bathe all winter long. Birds that find their food and water in one spot will naturally spend more time there. So regardless of the season, birdbaths make backyards more appealing to many birds.

Which leads to the second, and perhaps more important, reason to offer water in winter: Winter birdbaths attract more kinds and greater numbers of birds than feeders alone. My winter bath list includes bluebirds, Cedar Waxwings, robins, and Yellow-rumped Warblers, as well as most of my regular feeder birds. If I extend the list to include late fall, I can add Yellow Warblers, White-eyed Vireos, Scarlet Tanagers, Baltimore Orioles, Gray Catbirds, and Brown Thrashers.

To keep a winter bath busy and disease-free, fill it with fresh water daily, and scrub the bowl once a week. Even during winter, algae grows on mild, sunny days and can make a winter bath a scummy mess. It's also a good idea to scrub the heating element periodically, especially if your water is hard. Use vinegar or a product formulated to remove crusty deposits. Mineral-encrusted heaters operate less efficiently than clean ones.

HOW TO BUILD
A SIMPLE WATER FEATURE

With a little thought and effort, a birdbath can be a backyard highlight. Think habitat—pond, rocks, and aquatic plants—rather than just water.

A bird pond can be as simple or as extravagant as you care to make it. Begin by using a piece of rope to outline the size and shape you have in mind for the pool. Then dig it out to a depth of 10 to 12 inches. Slope the edges gently to the center of the pond so birds have a choice of water depth.

After excavating the pond, line it with layers of sand and gravel several inches deep. Then pour and shape 2 to 3 inches of concrete to create the actual pond. If you prefer, rather than concrete, which is heavy and difficult to work with, you can use a thick plastic liner, available at garden centers, to form the pond, placing the liner directly on top of the layer of sand. A third option is to buy a prefabricated pond. These are usually more than 6 inches deep, so you should add rocks to create shallow areas for bathing and drinking.

After the pond is in place, ring its perimeter with large, flat rocks; they hide the construction materials and give the pond a natural look. Then plant some native wildflowers around half the pond to add some color, and place a potted water lily or two into the water itself. Many garden centers now specialize in pools, ponds, and aquatic plants, so ask their aquatic specialists for advice on design and landscaping.

All that's left is the wait for birds to find the water. Eventually they will, but you can advertise a new pond by adding sound with a dripper or mister. Birds find the sound of moving water irresistible.

HOW TO BUILD A DUST BATH

Years ago, as I cruised a gravel road in central Oklahoma, a small cloud of dust up ahead caught my eye. I stopped about 50 yards away and focused my binoculars on the scene. Four Northern Bobwhites furiously fluffed their feathers and flailed their wings. They were bathing—in the dust.

Since then, I have seen Ruffed Grouse, Ring-necked Pheasants, Wild Turkeys, American Robins, Eastern Bluebirds, Northern Cardinals, Mourning Doves, and American Kestrels do the same thing. I have even seen House Wrens "bathing" in my kids' sandbox. These observations prompted me to designate a small space in my yard as a dust zone.

Building a dust bath is one of the easiest backyard bird projects you can tackle. Select an open, flat area with full exposure to sunlight. This ensures the area stays as dry as possible and minimizes the risk posed by stalking predators. An area 3 feet by 3 feet is adequate. Just remove the sod, and add the dust—equal parts sand and topsoil. Rim the perimeter with landscape timbers, bricks, or flat rocks. After a day or two of sunshine, your dust bath will be ready for dirty birds. As birds kick dust from the bath, it will be necessary to occasionally replenish the sand/soil mixture.

Dust bathing is most common during dry weather or in areas where standing water is in short supply. When water is unavailable, birds literally wallow in the dirt to stay clean.

A dusting bird typically squats and forms a small depression in the soil. Sometimes it pecks the surrounding soil and loosens it by scratching with its feet. The bird fluffs its feathers and uses its wings and feet to create a mini dust storm. Sometimes, a bird will actually roll in the dust. When finished, the bird stands, shakes its feathers, and preens with its bill. Oil gathered from the uropygial gland at the base of the tail conditions and waterproofs the feathers.

Dusting is just another way birds ensure that their feathers are kept in top condition. If feathers get too dry or too oily, they can deteriorate. Dusting may also soothe the irritations associated with molt and ectoparasites such as lice and mites.

Preening after dusting also helps align the individual barbs on the body's contour feathers, which increases the plumage's insulating and flight efficiency.

A dust bath is a simple, easy-to-build attraction that some birds find irresistible. Think of it as a solar-powered birdbath.

PART 4

NEST BOXES

THE "HOLE" STORY

Assemble a group of backyard birders, and sooner or later the conversation turns to new ways to attract more birds. So when Kathy Cain, one of the ringleaders of a small birding group near Parkersburg, West Virginia, mentioned "ghost trees," my ears perked up. Ghost trees, Kathy explained, are simply dead trees. I call them snags. Kathy said she had one in her backyard. "In fact, it is the centerpiece of my feeding station," she proudly claimed. "I hang feeders from its branches, and the birds just love it."

I've been a long-time proponent of backyard snags, so I found Kathy's testimonial fascinating. The big drawback, of course, is that neighbors often frown on dead trees. "What did your neighbors have to say when they realized you weren't going to remove an obviously dead tree?" I asked.

"Most accepted the idea after we explained its purpose, but it didn't die," Kathy replied. "We planted it."

Now I knew I had found a kindred spirit. Ten years ago I "planted" several small snags in my backyard in Stillwater, Oklahoma. I'm sure the neighbors are still talking about it. One assured me repeatedly that no matter how much I watered it, a dead tree wouldn't grow. But planting snags was the only way I knew to test their appeal to birds.

Back in the late 1970s, biologists began to appreciate the importance of snags in natural ecosystems. Woodpeckers (primary cavity nesters) excavate nest cavities in them and tear them apart in search of the insects that riddle their innards. In subsequent years, bluebirds, titmice, wrens, screech-owls, and kestrels (secondary cavity nesters) nest in the old woodpecker holes. Deer mice, flying squirrels, tree frogs, arboreal snakes and lizards, and myriad invertebrates also find shelter in abandoned cavities. Red-tailed Hawks perch on tall snags and scan the earth below for prey. Phoebes launch their fly-catching attacks from open branches on snags. Vultures roost on snags so they can bask in the early-morning sun to warm their bodies. And many songbirds, such as Indigo Buntings, cardinals, and bluebirds, sing from the tops of snags to advertise and defend their territories.

My fascination with snags and the birds they attract began in a meadow in southern Michigan in 1978. A single large snag in a brushy fencerow interrupted endless acres of corn- and hayfields. One June morning I watched three species tending active nests. High on the main trunk, a male kestrel delivered a meadow mouse to its mate. Forty feet below, a House Wren removed a fecal sac from its nest. And on the underside of a large, forking branch, a female Downy Woodpecker fed her brood. I've been hooked on snags ever since.

If cavities are such great places to nest, why do relatively few species nest in cavities? Only about eighty-five species of North American breeding birds use cavities. Here's the "hole" story.

It seems obvious that, compared to an open nest on the ground or in a tree, a cavity should provide better protection from the elements and predators for both the nestlings and the incubating adult. Cavities are well protected from rain and insulated from late-spring freezes and midsummer heat. And only predators small enough to enter the hole or strong enough to tear apart the cavity pose a threat.

Furthermore, cowbirds, which "parasitize" other birds' nests by laying their eggs in them, rarely choose the nests of cavity nesters. They prefer to pick on warblers, vireos, and native sparrows.

Does this protection translate to higher nest success? Yes. If measured as the percentage of nests that fledge at least one young bird, nest success is much higher among cavity nesters than open nesters. Nesting studies have shown that 60 to 80 percent of cavity nests succeed, while only 20 to 40 percent of open nests are successful.

But if cavities are such great places to nest, why don't all birds use them? Simply because cavities are usually in short supply—there are usually more pairs of cavity nesters than cavities. This leads to fierce competition for cavities and lots of time and energy spent defending nest sites. That's why it's so easy to get cavity nesters to use nest boxes placed in suitable habitat.

Also, birds require certain physical skills and behaviors to use cavities. Cavity nesters must have strong feet that can cling to the face of a cavity. And they must be curious and fearless about exploring dark holes and crevasses. Virtually all cavity nesters possess these traits. Open nesters do not.

Cavity nesters differ from open nesters in other ways, too. For example, they often nest early in the season. One incentive to nest early is to beat the post-winter emergence of black rat snakes. Rat snakes are excellent climbers and routinely search tree cavities for food. When they first appear in April, they tend to be sluggish and not terribly hungry. By June, however, they become a primary predator of cavity nestlings. If a bird gets a brood off before snakes get ravenous, it avoids a major predator.

Cavity nesters also take advantage of the security cavities provide by extending the brood-rearing period. Nestling bluebirds, chickadees, and wrens, for example, remain in the nest for sixteen to twenty-two days. Purple Martins remain nest bound for up to thirty days. Compare this to a nestling period of just ten to thirteen days for cardinals and robins. When open nesters leave the nest, they cannot fly and are extremely vulnerable to predators. The extra time in the nest permits young cavity nesters to leave the nest bigger, stronger, and more able to fly than their open-nesting counterparts.

Over a period of decades, a large, dead tree teems with all manner of life until natural decay takes its final toll. Then the snag topples to its final resting place. There, fungi and other decomposers return the stuff that trees are made of—organic matter and minerals—to the soil, where it can be reincorporated into new trees. By planting snags in our backyards, we can observe this entire process of death, rebirth, decay, and renewal.

My Oklahoma snag project was a smashing success. Heavy branches served as an ideal frame from which to hang feeders. And on cold days, when the feeders were constantly busy, scores of finches, chickadees, and titmice perched on the snag's branches as they waited their turns. One day a Sharp-shinned Hawk perched for ten minutes on the snag, hoping for an easy meal.

I was so sold on the notion of backyard snags that when I moved to my ridgetop home in northern West Virginia in 1985, I immediately planted a snag in the backyard. Once again, it quickly became the focal point of my feeding station.

But as I talked to Kathy Cain about her snag, I soon came to realize that my efforts were small potatoes. My snags were just 6 inches in diameter at eye level and 10 or 12 feet tall. Hers was huge—about 20 feet tall and 12 inches thick. Anchored in concrete, her snag will not fall until natural forces bring it down.

Just as I was ready to ask if I could visit her yard to see the ghost tree, Kathy mentioned that she got the idea from her friend Pam Moore, whose backyard snag in nearby Washington Bottom is even larger. Shortly after her husband, Tim, finished building their house, Pam asked him if he might be able to use 4x4 posts to build her an artificial tree. She suspected that such a structure would be a great place to hang feeders. He responded that it was certainly possible but suggested planting a real tree, reasoning that a snag would be more appealing than an artificial tree. The rest is history.

Sensing my interest in the backyard ghost tree phenomenon, Kathy mentioned that the Mountwood Bird Club was holding its next weekly outing at Pam's house. "Why don't you come and see for yourself?" she asked.

The following week I drove 90 miles south along the Ohio River to do just that. The temperature was mild, but it rained all morning long. I expected to see very few birds. When I arrived at Pam's house, her kitchen was already filled with local birders watching an impressive array of visitors at the feeders on her snag. And oh, what a snag it was. It towered at least 25 feet into the air and was at least 18 inches in diameter at eye level. Like Kathy's, Pam's snag was also anchored in concrete. Planting this ghost tree required a tractor, a pickup truck, a winch, and two men. In the distance, a second, smaller snag marked the far edge of the yard.

"Just watch for a few minutes, and you'll see how attractive birds find my ghost trees. I just hope the Brown Creeper shows up today," Pam said hopefully.

Over the next hour, a dozen species came and went to the feeders on the big snag. The House Finches, goldfinches, chickadees, and titmice were clearly regulars, but when a juvenile Yellow-bellied Sapsucker landed on the suet feeder, a brigade of binoculars went to work. And when a Brown Creeper visited the peanut butter feeder, several folks congratulated Pam on her prediction. "It comes every morning at about this time," she said. Even though my yard is nestled within a large wooded area, I've never had creepers come to my feeders.

Another highlight of that morning was a Carolina Wren that visited another peanut butter feeder—half an orange speared on a nail and filled with peanut butter. Over the course of the morning, it became obvious that Carolina Wrens and Brown Creepers love peanut butter.

Because the snag was so large and most of the branches were too high to reach, I asked Pam how she filled her feeders. Turns out she devised an ingenious system of hooks and poles that she uses to raise and lower even the highest feeders. She simply slips the pole under the feeder's hanger and lifts it off its perch. After filling the feeder, she uses the pole to replace the feeder on its hook.

Though food is clearly the focal point of Pam's ghost trees, it is by no means the only way she uses them. The family's Christmas tree was strapped to the base of the larger snag to provide cover for ground feeders. And several recently planted stems of ivy climbed the base of the snag, adding touches of both color and cover. A small hedge just a few feet from the snag provided additional escape cover that might prove crucial if a feral cat or hungry hawk showed up. A heated birdbath completed this ideal feeding station.

Pam emphasized that her snags attract birds all year long. "During the summer, when everything is green and lush, the snags really stand out. And all kinds of birds perch on them as they move through the yard."

A birdbath near a snag is a great way to attract species that don't often come to feeders. I've had great success attracting vireos, warblers, tanagers, and orioles to a birdbath. When the bath is located close to a snag, these colorful migrants often perch in the snag before bathing and then fly back to the same perch to preen and fluff their feathers.

Another way to improve the spring and summer appeal of a backyard snag is to plant trumpet honeysuckle (*Lonicera sempervirens*) or trumpet creeper (*Campsis radicans*) at its base. These vines' nectar-rich flowers attract hummingbirds all summer long.

If a snag is large enough, woodpeckers may actually excavate a hole and nest in the tree. Then you'll have a natural cavity for wrens, chickadees, or bluebirds in future years. Susan and Richard Day of Alma, Illinois, had exactly this experience. A pair of Red-headed Woodpeckers excavated a cavity and nested in a snag they planted in their yard. Not only did they get to enjoy watching the family life of these magnificent birds, but Richard also managed to take a series of stunning photographs documenting the whole nesting process.

A snag also makes an ideal post for hanging a nest box. Bluebirds, chickadees, and wrens will use small boxes hung 4 to 6 feet high in suitable habitat, while screech-owls and kestrels are easily coaxed into larger boxes hung 12 to 15 feet above the ground. Selecting the right snag simply requires walking through the woods until you find one you like. If you don't own a woodlot, be sure to ask permission before trespassing and removing the snag. A few words explaining why you want the snag usually guarantees permission, if only so the landowner can watch "one of those crazy bird-watchers" harvest a dead tree.

I prefer snags that have several stout horizontal branches from which I can hang feeders. The only general rule of snag selection is that bigger is better. But remember, the bigger the snag, the more difficult it will be to transport and "plant."

Planting a snag is theoretically simple. Just be sure to have several people, a winch, and at least one truck or tractor available. Dig a hole 4 to 6 feet deep and about 8 inches wider than the diameter of the base. Hoist the snag into place, anchor it with a few braces, and fill the hole with concrete. Make sure the snag is vertical before the concrete sets.

At first, the idea of landscaping with dead trees may seem laughable. But an understanding of snag ecology, especially their importance to birds, can make the difference between an eyesore and a thing of beauty. In winter, flocks of colorful birds visit snags that support entire feeding stations. In the spring, Indigo Buntings and cardinals sing their hearts out from the highest branches and woodpeckers may excavate nesting cavities. In the summer, hummingbirds mob the honeysuckle that embraces the towering skeleton. And in the fall, flocks of migrants may perch and rest as they prepare for the long trip south. There's little doubt that a prominent snag can spell success for any backyard birder.

CHOOSING THE BEST NEST BOX

There is nothing more rewarding than peeking out the window on a warm spring morning and seeing a bird carry nesting material to a nest box. You know you have made a difference. If that nest box, which you built or bought, was not there, that bird might not nest this year. You have helped a cavity-nesting bird and ensured yourself a ringside seat to a show that will last the entire nesting season.

Some folks offer nest boxes just for bluebirds. If other cavity nesters use their nest boxes, they feel cheated or at least disappointed. Others, and I am among this group, adopt an equal-opportunity housing philosophy. While bluebirds are welcome at any of my nest boxes, I enjoy Tree Swallows, Carolina Chickadees, Tufted Titmice, White-breasted Nuthatches, Carolina and House Wrens, and Great-crested Flycatchers with equal enthusiasm. In fact, because nuthatches and flycatchers rarely use my nest boxes, I probably get more excited about these birds than about bluebirds.

Nest boxes provide a secure nest site to a variety of cavity-nesting birds. Some might be more popular than others, but all are fascinating to watch as they go through the stages of the nesting cycle: nest building, egg laying, incubation, hatching, brood rearing, and fledging. So if a Tree Swallow moves into the nest box you intended for bluebirds, enjoy the swallows and put up another nest box—or another dozen.

Sometimes it seems there are as many designs for nest boxes as there are people who make them. Are some better than others? If so, why? Which is best? After a few seasons of casually putting up a few nest boxes and monitoring them occasionally, these are the questions more experienced backyard birders ask.

Several types of nest boxes have become popular with both birds and birders. I will describe four styles that are either easily built or available commercially and assess their advantages and disadvantages. Though field tests have been going on for years, none can yet be crowned the *best,* though many birders champion their favorite style.

That's where you come in. Step beyond simply watching the birds that use your nest boxes. Study them. Keep notes. Record data. Even if you have neither the time nor the inclination to analyze the results, there are lots of professional and amateur ornithologists who would welcome your data.

You need not be an ornithologist to collect important information. Margaret Morse Nice, for example, was a child psychologist. In her spare time she earned the respect and admiration of American ornithology with her landmark studies of Song Sparrows.

Cavity-nesting birds—those that use nest boxes—are ideally suited to simple basic research. You never have to search for a nest, and the work can be completed in your backyard. Even in a small backyard, pairs of nest boxes can be erected side by side. If you provide the opportunity, the birds will choose the style of nest box they prefer. You compile the results and become part of a continental research project.

To participate in nationwide research on nest boxes, contact Cornell University's Laboratory of Ornithology, Nest Box Network, 159 Sapsucker Woods Road, Ithaca, NY 14850.

Because bluebirds are by far most people's favorite cavity nester, and because low bluebird populations back in the 1950s and 1960s spawned today's continuing interest in nest boxes, most nest boxes are designed for bluebirds. The critical element in a bluebird house is hole size: A $1^{1}/_{2}$-inch-hole admits Eastern Bluebirds but usually keeps European Starlings out. Few cavity nesters, however, understand our intent, so bluebird houses tend to be used by any cavity nesters that find them comfortable.

All good nest boxes share several qualities:

- They should be built of wood at least $^{3}/_{4}$ inch thick. This insulates the interior from late-spring chills and midsummer heat. Boxes constructed of recycled plastic or concrete also work, but they are expensive.
- They should *not* have a perch. All cavity nesters have strong feet and can acrobatically climb on virtually any wooden surface. Perches just give House Sparrows a place from which to defend the nest box.
- They should be assembled with galvanized screws or nails. Ordinary nails and screws rust, and the nest boxes deteriorate more quickly.
- They must be able to be opened for periodic monitoring and cleaning. Otherwise, nesting material accumulates, mice move in, and the box becomes unusable. I prefer nest boxes that open from the front or side.

- They should not be built of treated lumber.
- They should not be painted on the inside. Earth-tone paints, stains, or water sealers on the exterior are OK but not necessary.
- They need not have any sort of escape ladder built into the box for the nestlings to use to fledge. When young cavity nesters are ready to leave the nest, they are well developed and can easily reach the hole to fledge. Nest boxes used by swallows and ducks are the exception to this rule. Tree Swallows, in particular, migrate north early in the spring and are often caught by late-winter or early-spring cold snaps. Such conditions send their flying insect prey into hiding, and swallows often seek shelter in nest boxes until warmer weather returns. If the nest box has no escape ladder (a piece of hardware cloth or a series of grooves cut inside the box just beneath the hole), weakened swallows may be unable to leave the box when conditions improve. Boxes intended for Wood Ducks and other cavity-nesting waterfowl require an escape ladder so day-old hatchlings can climb out of the cavity.
- The roof should extend at least 3 inches beyond the front of the box to protect the interior from driving rain.
- The floor should have several $1/4$-inch drain holes to prevent flooding during windy rainstorms.
- Near the top of the box, there should be ventilation holes or slots to permit warm air to rise and escape on hot summer days.
- The top of the $1\frac{1}{2}$-inch entrance hole should be about 1 inch from the top.

BASIC BOX

The basic box is a simple square, vertical nest box that measures 4 or 5 inches square and 10 to 12 inches deep. It opens from the front, side, or top. The roof may be flat or pitched.

The major advantages of the basic box are that it is cheap and easy to make. I can easily get ten from a single sheet of $3/4$-inch exterior plywood. The major disadvantage, and this applies to all vertically oriented nest boxes, is that cavity nesters tend to build their nest up to the hole, thus making it easy for predators to reach in and grab the contents.

SLOT BOX

Dr. Wayne Davis, a University of Kentucky ornithologist, designed a bluebird box with a horizontal opening rather than a circular hole. He found that

Eastern Bluebirds preferred the slot box to conventional nest boxes. More importantly, European Starlings avoided the slot boxes when the slot was 3 centimeters wide. The entrance slot is formed by simply lowering the front of the box 3 centimeters from the roof. Bluebirds enter and exit the box through the slot.

The slot box is a simple variation on the basic box theme, with the slot replacing the hole. Hence, it is easy to build and inexpensive. Like the basic box, however, the slot box is vulnerable to predators such as raccoons, cats, and opossums.

PETERSON BOX

The Peterson box was designed by Minnesota bluebirder Dick Peterson. From the side, this box is V-shaped; therefore, the area at the base of the box is smaller than the area at the top. One consequence of this design is that less nesting material is needed. The roof is steeply pitched to discourage predators. And the entrance hole is elliptically shaped to discourage starlings.

The Peterson box is highly regarded among bluebirders who have tried it. I have used several at my house for the last three years, and they are usually occupied. In a field test, Wayne Davis found that Kentucky bluebirds strongly preferred the Peterson box to any other style.

The only disadvantage of the Peterson box is that the design is fairly complicated, and it is relatively difficult to build. A novice do-it-yourselfer might find the Peterson box a challenge.

Peterson Box

TREE BRANCH NEST BOX

Frank Zuern, a Wisconsin bluebirder, came up with the tree branch nest box after hearing tales of bluebirds nesting in hollow horizontal tree branches and seeing a pair of bluebirds nesting in the barrel of a cannon on a Civil War battlefield in Georgia. Zuern designed a horizontal bluebird nest box—an

A nest box with a 1 1/2-inch hole admits Eastern Bluebirds and keeps European Starlings out.

All birds, such as this Northern Cardinal, need drinking water year-round.

Chickadees are among many birds who eat black oil sunflower seeds.

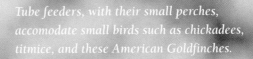
Tube feeders, with their small perches,
accomodate small birds such as chickadees,
titmice, and these American Goldfinches.

Nest boxes should be moved every few years and guarded to minimize predation.

A ruby-throated hummingbird and trumpet creeper.

Suet is a good source of fat and protein, which is especially valuable to birds, such as this Downy Woodpecker, during cold winter months.

Snow-covered brush provides safe cover for an American Tree Sparrow.

Live treats will attract virtually all backyard birds. Here, a Carolina Wren enjoys mealworms.

An electric submersible heater, available from most birding stores, will make your bird bath a popular drinking oasis for birds in freezing weather.

Male and female Evening Grosbeaks in hawthorn.

A birch snag attracts a Red-bellied Woodpecker.

A male Cardinal perches in forsythia, a colorful sight in a backyard bird garden.

artificial hollow branch. The inside dimensions are $3^1/2$ inches wide, 5 inches high, and 16 inches long. It mounts directly on a fence post, and as long as birds place their nest at the far end of the artificial branch, it is safe from predators.

This ingenious design is still being tested, but the preliminary results are encouraging. Most nest boxes are made resistant to predators with baffles placed above and/or below the box. The tree branch box seems, by virtue of its design, to be reasonably predator resistant. In early tests, although many boxes had claw marks on them, no mammalian predators destroyed any nests.

The downside to the tree branch nest box is that, like the Peterson box, the plans are relatively complicated. In both cases, however, it seems a small price to pay for nest boxes whose designs seem so successful and attractive to cavity nesters.

FIELD TESTING NEST BOXES

You may want to consider a nest box testing program of your own. Erect boxes in pairs. For example, match a basic box to a Peterson box at one end of the yard, and place a tree branch nest box and a slot box at the other. Even just a few experimental pairings can produce meaningful results. Visit the nest boxes regularly, perhaps once or twice a week. Prepare a data sheet and record the date, time of visit, contents of nest box, and other pertinent observations. By the end of the nesting season, you'll have a body of information to analyze, interpret, and present to the local bird club.

One word of warning: Birds are creatures of habit. Adults typically choose similar nest sites from year to year, and first-time nesters often select a nest site similar to the one in which they were raised. Consequently, birds familiar with one type of nest box may seem reluctant to use a new style of nest box, even though testing elsewhere suggests that the new design might be better. This is why field testing must be completed over a period of years. By conducting a multiyear test, you may be able to document a shift in preference from one type of nest box to another.

Detailed plans for the basic box, the slot box, and the Peterson box can be found in a pull-out supplement to *Bluebirds Forever,* by Connie Toops (Voyager Press, 1994). For tree branch nest box plans, see the Winter 1994 issue of *Sialia,* the quarterly journal of the North American Bluebird Society, P.O. Box 74, Darlington, WI 53530. NABA's publication is now called *Bluebird Magazine.*

SPECIES	Interior Floor Size of Box (inches)	Interior Height of Box (inches)	Entrance Hole Diameter (inches)	Mount Box this High (feet)
Chickadees	4x4	9-12	1 $^{1}/_{8}$-1 $^{1}/_{2}$	5-15
Prothonotary & Lucy's warblers	4x4	12	1 $^{1}/_{4}$	5-12
Titmice	4x4	12	1 $^{1}/_{2}$	5-12
White-breasted Nuthatch	4x4	12	1 $^{1}/_{2}$	5-12
Carolina Wren	4x4	9-12	1-1 $^{1}/_{2}$	5-10
Eastern Bluebird	4x4	12	1 $^{1}/_{2}$	5-6
Western Bluebird	5x5	12	1 $^{1}/_{2}$-1 $^{9}/_{16}$	5-6
Mountain Bluebird	5x5	12	1 $^{9}/_{16}$	5-6
Tree Swallow	5x5	10-12	1 $^{1}/_{2}$	5-10
Violet-green Swallow	5x5	10-12	1 $^{1}/_{2}$	5-10
Purple Martin	6x6	6	2 $^{1}/_{8}$	15-25
Great-crested Flycatcher	6x6	12	1 $^{3}/_{4}$-2	6-20
Ash-throated Flycatcher	6x6	12	1 $^{3}/_{4}$-2	6-20
House Finch	5x5	10	1 $^{1}/_{2}$	5-10
Downy Woodpecker	4x4	12	1 $^{1}/_{2}$	5-20
Hairy Woodpecker	6x6	14	1 $^{1}/_{2}$	8-20
Red-bellied Woodpecker	6x6	14	2	8-20
Golden-fronted Woodpecker	6x6	14	2	8-20
Red-headed Woodpecker	6x6	14	2	8-20
Northern Flicker	7x7	16-24	2 $^{1}/_{2}$	10-20
Pileated Woodpecker	12x12	24	4	15-25
Bufflehead	7x7	17	3	5-15
Wood Duck	12x12	24	3x4	5-20
Hooded Merganser	12x12	24	3x4	5-30
Goldeneyes	12x12	24	3 $^{1}/_{4}$x4 $^{1}/_{4}$	15-20
Common Merganser	12x12	24	5x6	8-20
Saw-whet Owl	7x7	12	2 $^{1}/_{2}$	8-20
Screech-owls	8x8	18	3	8-30
Boreal Owl	8x8	18	3	8-30
Barred Owl	14x14	28	8	15-30
Barn Owl	12x36	16	6x7	15-30
American Kestrel	9x9	16-18	3	12-30

For All Nest Boxes: Interior height listed above refers to inside back panel. Always baffle nest boxes. Sizes
For Wren Boxes: Larger, oblong holes make it easier to get twigs into box.
For Swallow Boxes: Carve grooves, or place hardware cloth on inside of front of box.
For Purple Martins: Size listed here is for one compartment in a multi-unit martin house. See *Enjoying*
For Duck Boxes: Add 3" of wood chips to floor of box. Staple 5"-wide hardware cloth "ladder" directly
For Woodpecker Boxes: Pack cavity full with wood chips and sawdust.
For Owl Boxes: Add 3" of wood chips to floor of box.
Reprinted from A Guide to Bird Homes *by Scott Shalaway, published by Bird Watcher's Digest Press (PO Box 110*

CAVITY-NESTING BIRDS

Habitat for Box Placement	Comments
Open woods and edges	A 1 1/8" hole excludes all other birds except House Sparrows.
Wooded swamps and streams	Mount box on a metal pole 5 to 8 feet above open water.
Wooded areas and edge habitat	A 1 1/8" hole excludes all other birds except House Sparrows.
Wooded areas and edge habitat	Other nuthatch species may prefer a 1 1/4" hole.
Old fields and thickets	House Wrens (1" hole) and Bewick's Wrens (1 1/4" hole).
Open land with scattered trees	See *Enjoying Bluebirds More,* published by BWD Press.
Open land with scattered trees	
Open meadows above 5,000 feet	
Open land near pond or lake	Place escape ladder on inside front of box. See below.
Pastures, fields, parks	
Open country near water	Entrance hole 1" above the floor. See comments below.
Open woods and edges	Use a 1 9/16" hole if starlings are a problem.
Open, semi-arid country	
Backyards and porches	Often nests in hanging plants.
Forest openings and edges	
Forest openings and edges	
Forest openings and edges	
Forest openings and edges	
Forest openings and edges	
Farmland, open country	
Mature forest	
Wooded lakeshores, swamps	
Wooded swamps, bottomland	Hole is a horizontally oriented oval.
Wooded swamps, bottomland	
Wooded lakeshores, swamps	
Wooded lakeshores, swamps	
Forest clearings and edges	
Farmland, orchards, woods	
Boreal forests and bogs	
Mature bottomland forest	
Open farmland, marshes	Place box high in barn, silo. Hole should be 4" above floor.
Farmland	

above are minimum ideal sizes for each species.

Purple Martins More.
under hole on inside of box. Mount boxes higher when not placed over water.

Marietta, OH 45750. 800-879-2473. www.birdwatchersdigest.com).

HOW TO BUILD A NATURAL-LOOKING NEST BOX

One of the nice things about most cavity-nesting birds is that they use just about any secure artificial cavity we provide them. We humans, on the other hand, are sometimes harder to please. I've heard complaints that wooden nest boxes are too plain or even boring, and some folks want a more natural look. Or maybe you are a photographer and you would like your nest boxes to look more like natural cavities. If you are among those in search of a more natural look, here are some tips.

Existing nest boxes can be given a natural makeover by simply tacking a slab of bark over the front of the nest box. If the bark has a suitable-size hole that can be superimposed over the nest box's hole, great. If not, just chisel out a hole at the appropriate spot on the bark. Work carefully so the hole does not appear artificial. When you take photographs, you can simply zoom in on the slab and crop out the obviously man-made parts of the nest box.

If you prefer nest boxes with a completely natural look, you have several options. Mills that cut raw trees into boards often throw away or burn the outer slabs of bark they remove from the logs. Many mills practically give away this by-product; some actually do give it away. In your woodworking shop, the slabs can be cut to size and used to build nest boxes just like ordinary boards. Assemble with the bark to the outside, and you have a great looking natural nest box.

Another option is to find some hollow logs in the woodpile or in the woods (be sure you have permission from the landowner to collect them). Cut the logs to 12-inch lengths (18 inches for kestrels, screech-owls, and flickers), drill appropriate entrance holes about an inch from the top, and equip the bottom with a floor that fits snugly inside the log. This prevents rainwater from creeping up into the cavity via capillary action. Finally, hinge a slab on the top of the cavity, making sure it extends beyond the sides by at least a $1/2$ inch and beyond the front by 3 inches. That, in a nutshell, is a top-opening, hollow log nest box.

The most natural of nest boxes requires a lot of work but looks great. Split a solid 12-inch log, then make like a woodpecker and chisel out a nesting cavity. Allowing for 1-inch-thick walls and a 4-inch-diameter cavity, the log should be at least 6 inches thick. Leave 2 inches of wood at both the top and bottom of the cavity. When the cavity has been completed, hinge the halves of the log together at the bottom, and drill an entrance hole at the top of the cavity on the front piece. Cover the top with a slab of bark fastened to the back piece, and you've got a front-opening, natural nesting log and a much greater appreciation for woodpeckers' role in maintaining a continuing supply of natural cavities.

Natural nest boxes are definitely more difficult to build than conventional nest boxes, but by creating a wild look that photographers and many birds find irresistible, they are worth the effort.

THE COST OF PROVIDING HOUSING FOR BIRDS

How much is a bluebird worth? That may seem a curious query, but for those of us who monitor nest boxes, it's a valid question. Economics—costs and benefits—plays a critical role in wildlife conservation. A few years ago, I managed to put a price on the heads of some cavity-nesting birds.

One of the reasons cavity-nesting birds use cavities is because they are relatively safe from predators. Nest boxes, which are simply man-made cavities, are just as safe as natural cavities, so bluebirds, chickadees, wrens, and Tree Swallows often use them. In nature there is a steady supply of new cavities, thanks to woodpeckers and decay. The annual supply of new cavities tends to be randomly distributed, so predators must constantly search for them. Nest boxes, on the other hand, last for many years and can always be found in the same place. Predators, especially raccoons, eventually figure this out and return regularly to familiar nest boxes. In this way, nest boxes often become predator feeders after just a few years.

Learning this lesson has taken years of fieldwork and experience. I finally questioned the wisdom of maintaining a trail of fifty progressively less successful nest boxes. Maybe I ought to concentrate on fewer boxes and try to make them predator proof, I reasoned. So I invested $400 to create ten predator-proof nest boxes. I bought ten treated, 4x4x8-foot posts ($8 each) and ten heavy-duty predator baffles ($30 each), and I built ten nest boxes at a cost of about $2 each.

I picked ten locations that bluebirds or chickadees have used in the past, dug post holes, and placed the baffles on the posts beneath the boxes. Over the course of the nesting season, the results were phenomenal. Bluebirds or chickadees used seven of the ten predator-proof boxes. One set of bluebird eggs never hatched, but the other six nests all fledged chicks. Nest boxes had occupied these locations for nine years, so older, experienced raccoons and rat snakes surely knew their locations. Yet predation dropped to zero.

The key to this success is the predator baffle. A variety of styles are commercially available, but many are cheap and flimsy. I chose those made by Erva Tool & Die Co. in Chicago. The baffle is a 28-inch-long cylinder made of heavy sheet metal. The top has a round or square hole to accommodate either a 4x4 post or a round metal pipe. The 7-inch-diameter cylinder prevents predators from climbing over the baffle; the closed top prevents them from climbing directly up the post. I selected Erva baffles because they are heavy and well made. I expect them to last at least ten years.

All this sounds fine, you say, but isn't $400 a lot to invest in just ten nest boxes? It certainly is—if you simply look at it as a one-time cost and benefit. But I see this as a long-term investment. I estimate very conservatively that each unit will last at least ten years. Immediately that reduces my cost to $40 per year, or $4 per box per year. Furthermore, assuming that seven boxes will be used each year and that each used box will produce five chicks (a reasonable average), the annual cost of producing bluebirds and chickadees works out to $1.14 per individual. Finally, bluebirds usually nest at least twice each year, so the cost of producing bluebirds in boxes used twice each season drops to a bit more than 50 cents per bluebird. If birds use more than seven boxes, and an occasional bluebird raises three broods, the per bird cost drops even more.

One of the most challenging problems in the business of conservation is attaching a price tag to wildlife. I'm no economist, but I think that's what I've just done. If bluebirds and chickadees cost between 50 cents and $1 to produce, I'm willing to pay that price to ensure that they can nest safely and successfully on my property. In my mind, it's a bargain.

PROTECTING NEST BOXES FROM PREDATORS AND COMPETITORS

Putting up a nest box or two and then watching a pair of bluebirds or chickadees raise their brood sounds appealing to almost anyone interested in birds. It personalizes wildlife science. The prospect of helping wild birds reproduce is also probably responsible for pushing many birders into the world of nest boxes and cavity-nesting birds. Unfortunately, many beginners think that after they have put up a nest box or two, their job is done. In reality, their responsibility has just begun.

The purpose of erecting nest boxes is to provide a safe, secure nest site for cavity nesters such as bluebirds, Tree Swallows, chickadees, titmice, nuthatches, wrens, screech-owls, and kestrels. During the first few years of a nest box's life, it usually meets these expectations. It almost seems too easy. A trail of ten nest boxes, for example, might produce six to eight successful nests during its first two or three years if it is located in suitable habitat. (A successful nest is one from which at least one nestling fledges.)

During the fourth or fifth year, however, nest success usually drops dramatically. After a few years, predators such as raccoons, squirrels, snakes, cats, and opossums recognize nest boxes as feeding stations, places to come for a succulent meal of fresh eggs or tasty chicks. If you fail to acknowledge and act upon this knowledge, you may as well not put up nest boxes in the first place.

Let's begin by reviewing the antagonists in this ecological drama of predator and prey. Most are mammals—raccoons, squirrels, chipmunks, opossums, cats, martens, and others. Raccoons are by far the most notorious and widespread. Thanks to their size, strength, intelligence, and sheer physical abilities, they are most cavity nesters' worst nightmare. Some predators, most notably starlings, jays, and crows, are other birds. They are particularly troublesome because they get to the nest box from above.

In some parts of the country, snakes can be even more devastating than raccoons. Across the southern two-thirds of the United States, for example, rat snakes are abundant. They are excellent climbers and eat eggs and chicks regularly. In the plains states, the same can be said of gopher or bull snakes. It is important to keep in mind that snakes visit nest boxes and even use them for shelter from time to time, because snakes are the one predator you are likely to actually find in a nest box. After consuming the contents of a nest, a snake is usually too large to leave through the entrance hole, so it will rest in the nest box until its meal digests. This can take a week or longer. Nothing is more startling than opening a nest box expecting to find a nest full of chicks, only to discover a 4-foot-long rat snake. (Rat and gopher snakes are nonpoisonous and harmless to man, so please do not kill them. Leave them alone, or move them to another area.)

HOW TO PREDATOR-PROOF A NEST BOX

Your primary objective as a nest box landlord should not be to destroy predators, but to make nest boxes as resistant to them as possible. One way to satisfy that primary objective is to use predator-resistant nest box designs. The steeply pitched roof of the Peterson nest box apparently makes it difficult for predators to reach the entrance hole. Likewise, the distance to the nesting chamber in the horizontally oriented tree branch nest box seems to effectively put nests out of reach of most predators. So the best advice for someone just beginning a nest box trail is to start with field-tested, predator-resistant designs. Experienced trail operators, however, may find it too expensive and time-consuming to replace all the nest boxes on a conservation trail. The challenge in these circumstances is to make existing nest boxes, regardless of their design, more resistant to predators.

The first step is to fasten nest boxes on free-standing poles rather than on fence posts or trees. Fence post– and tree-mounted nest boxes are easy to get to from above. A pole-mounted nest box must be approached from below by most predators.

Predation can be reduced greatly by mounting each nest box on a smooth metal pole, coating the pole with silicone spray or grease, and attaching a baffle immediately beneath the nest box. A baffle is a sheet metal barrier hung just below the nest box to prevent climbing predators from reaching the nest. It may be a large, shallow, inverted cone 36 inches in diameter or a 6- to 8-inch-diameter cylinder that's at least 24 inches tall. When baffling nest boxes, bigger is better.

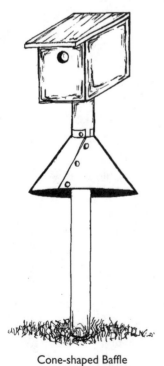

Cone-shaped Baffle

Both styles of baffles are readily available commercially. If you just need a few baffles, buying them is easier than making them. If you've got lots of nest boxes to protect, however, it's much cheaper to build your own.

To build a shallow cone, cut a 36-inch-diameter piece of sheet metal, and punch a hole in the center large enough to accommodate the mounting pole. Then use tin snips to make a straight cut from the outer edge to the center. Now pull the two free edges together so they overlap slightly, and screw or rivet them together. The cone shape results when the edges are overlapped.

A cylindrical baffle requires only a length of stovepipe and some $^1/_2$-inch hardware cloth. Cut a circle of hardware cloth that's just a bit larger than the inside diameter of the stovepipe. Then cut a small hole in the center of the wire mesh to

accommodate the mounting pole, and bend the edges of the hardware cloth downward so it just fits inside the pipe about 1 inch from the top. Now cut three or four equally spaced, 1-inch-wide, 1-inch-deep tabs around the top of the pipe. Bend these tabs down to secure the hardware cloth from above.

Support either type of baffle by bolting together two pieces of hanger irons just below the nest box. Baffles will wobble freely on this support piece and discourage predators from attempting to bypass the baffle.

If nest boxes are hung in the woods for chickadees, titmice, and nuthatches, baffles have limited value because access from above is so easy. Consider this before starting a woodland nest box trail. In open bluebird habitat, however, baffles can reduce predation to almost zero.

Another simple way to reduce predation is with predator guards. One type is simply an extra thickness of wood placed directly over the entrance hole. By increasing the dis-

Stovepipe Baffle

tance across which predators must reach, you add a small measure of safety to any nest. Though some experienced nest box operators pooh-pooh this simple device, it provides at least a small margin of safety and certainly does no harm.

The Noel predator guard, named for its designer, Jim Noel, is a wire mesh cage placed around the entrance hole. Birds are unbothered by the wire cage, which extends about 5 inches beyond the hole, but it creates a serious obstacle for predators.

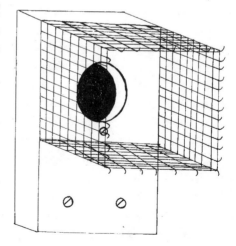

Noel Predator Guard

Complete nest box plans are available from the following:

Simple front-opening slot box
Richard Tuttle
311 West Central Ave.
Delaware, OH 43015
(Include $1 for postage and handling)

Peterson box
Bluebird Recovery Program
Audubon Chapter of Minneapolis
P.O. Box 3801
Minneapolis, MN 55403

(Send a tax-deductible donation of $5 for membership and box pattern)

See also pull-out supplement to *Bluebird Forever* by Connie Toops (Voyager Press, 1994).

Another antipredator strategy experienced nest box operators can try is relocating nest boxes every few years. Predators are creatures of habit and return to known food sources. That's why nest box success tends to decline over time.

A 100-nest-box trail that has been up for five years or more becomes more of a raccoon feeder than a tool to enhance the production of cavity-nesting birds. By relocating nest boxes to an alternate set of poles, predators must rediscover the nest boxes—and that takes time. During that learning period, however long it lasts, relocated nest boxes are safer than unmoved ones.

In a Scandinavian ornithological journal, G. A. Sonerud reported that relocated Tengmalm's Owl nest boxes were much more successful than nest boxes that remained in one place for many years. In one trial, relocated nest boxes suffered only 22 percent predation, while unmoved nest boxes had an 83 percent predation rate. Given those impressive numbers, I think relocating nest boxes as an antipredator strategy is certainly worth some study here in North America.

The most challenging part of a nest box relocation study is that it is a long-term project. Since most university graduate students try to finish their programs in two to four years, long-term projects are ideal for serious amateurs. One of the beauties of ornithology is its rich history of contributions by amateurs.

NEST BOX COMPETITORS

Perhaps the most universal threat to cavity nesters using nest boxes is not a predator, but the House Sparrow. These ubiquitous pests are not native to North America; they were introduced back in the mid-1800s.

House Sparrows are especially abundant in agricultural areas, where they aggressively compete with native cavity nesters for nest sites. Their habits include breaking and removing other birds' eggs, killing incubating adults, and building their own nests on top of the carcasses of the original occupants of the cavity. Because bluebirds prefer similar open habitats, bluebirds are frequent victims, but I have seen chickadees and Bewick's Wrens killed or evicted from nest boxes by House Sparrows.

It is virtually impossible to exclude House Sparrows from a nest box by reducing hole size. I have watched them squeeze, at first tentatively and then easily, through a $^7/_8$-inch hole. Hence, House Sparrow control becomes a time-consuming and distasteful part of nest box management. Because they are not native to the United States, House Sparrows are unprotected by state or federal laws. They may be trapped or killed at will. Sparrow traps available at most hardware stores can catch many birds in one setting, though *it is essential to check the trap regularly and release native species that might also get caught.*

Another option is to turn a nest box into a sparrow trap by adding a special trapdoor mechanism. Though trapping and killing House Sparrows may seem cruel, it often becomes necessary if a nest box trail is to succeed. Incubating females can easily be trapped on the nest at night. Controlling males is more important, however, because they "own" the nest box. Remove a female, and the male simply recruits a new mate. Remove a male, and the female moves on.

In any case, monitor nest boxes regularly, and remove all House Sparrow eggs and nests. Their nests are easy to recognize. Nesting materials include an untidy collection of grass, feathers, and assorted litter. Many House Sparrow nests also have nesting material arched up over the cup, giving the nest a domed appearance.

Controlling House Sparrows comes down to a battle of wills between bird and man. They can rebuild a nest in a day or two, so you must simply be more persistent than they. The reward for your determination will be significantly greater nest box use and success by native cavity nesters.

European Starlings, another unprotected import, pose similar problems, but because they are larger birds, they usually cannot enter bluebird-size nest boxes. They can, however, wreak havoc on Purple Martin houses and larger nest boxes intended for screech-owls, American Kestrels, and Wood Ducks. Treat starlings like House Sparrows; eliminate them any way you can.

UNDERSTANDING PREDATION

Birds fall prey to tooth and talon every day. Bird-watchers—especially those of us who attract birds to our backyards—witness predation regularly. Predators learn to visit our feeding stations, birdbaths, and nest boxes for easy meals. Because we love birds and usually believe that more birds are better than fewer birds, predators often suffer society's slings and arrows.

It is easy to vilify raccoons, squirrels, climbing snakes, and feral cats, but let's not ignore birds that eat other birds. Sharp-shinned and Cooper's Hawks and American Kestrels frequently prey on feeder birds. Jays, crows, magpies, and owls are ferocious predators of nesting birds. Brown-headed and Bronzed Cowbirds limit the populations of other species, not by killing them directly, but by laying their eggs in other birds' nests. Growing cowbirds monopolize the food parents bring to the nest, and often the host chicks die. This "brood parasitism" takes a devastating toll on warblers, vireos, and native sparrows every year.

Predation and death are natural parts of the cycle of life. Everyone can tell at least one story about predators killing baby birds. It might concern a robin nest in a tree outside the living room window. Or perhaps it involved a brood of phoebes nesting on the front porch. Even veteran birders and biologists can take such losses hard. I know I have. In Oklahoma one summer a rat snake ate four sixteen-day-old bluebird nestlings just days away from fledging. Here in West Virginia, a raccoon wiped out a brood of one of the few White-breasted Nuthatches that ever used one of my nest boxes. (This was before I wised up and hung metal baffles under my nest boxes.) Several years ago I stood stunned and fascinated when a Sharp-shinned Hawk careened around the corner of the house and picked a hummingbird out of midair. The hummer screamed as predator and prey disappeared into the woods.

A more detailed account illustrates the determined resiliency birds can display when harassed by predators. In 1983, while living in Oklahoma, I found a freshly built Carolina Chickadee nest in one of my nest boxes. Over the course of three months, I experienced a predictable series of highs and lows.

March 10. An inch of fresh green moss covers the nest box floor. Three days later, the mossy base is 3 inches thick, and the inner cup is lined with opossum fur.

March 21. The eight-egg clutch is complete. In just eight days, the female has put out more than half her body weight in eggs.

April 4. I approach the nest box to see if the eggs have hatched and I notice an adult chickadee enter the box. I cover the hole, open the door just enough to slide my hand inside, and gently grab the bird on the nest. It is the female, and she is brooding eight tiny, just-hatched nestlings. I band and weigh her (she weighs 10.5 grams, about $^1/_3$ ounce), and then return her to the nest. She nestles right down, not minding the disturbance one bit.

April 16. I band the entire twelve-day-old brood. They now look like miniature chickadees, though they still have tufts of down sticking up from their heads, and their tail feathers have not yet fully emerged. I'm feeling mighty proud.

April 23. When I make my rounds, I see some nesting material protruding from the hole. My heart sinks. The chicks are gone; the nest has been torn apart. Most likely a raccoon reached in and pulled the chicks out, one by one. A wonderful meal for the raccoon, but a tragedy for the chickadees. Coincidentally, I discover a new chickadee nest in a nest box about 100 yards from the other. The nest is complete and already contains two eggs.

May 7. I return to the box containing the new chickadee nest, reach in, and grab the incubating female. The fur-lined cup cradles six eggs, and the female is already banded. She is the female from the first nest. Allowing time for nest building and egg laying, she lost her first brood shortly after my visit on April 16. She wasted no time and immediately renested. All six eggs hatch later in the month, and in early June six chicks fledge. Such are the joys and heartbreaks that keep the study of nesting birds irresistible.

Whether we witness predation directly or only find the telltale evidence, it seems devastating. Even if we understand the "big picture," we wonder if our local birds can withstand the never-ending onslaught. Usually they can, thanks to their surprising longevity and tenacious breeding habits.

Banding records reveal that most birds, even small songbirds, can live surprisingly long. Among backyard birds, Black-capped Chickadees have lived as long as twelve years; House Wrens, seven years; Red-bellied Woodpeckers, twenty years; American Robins, eleven years; Northern Cardinals, thirteen years; Dark-eyed Juncos, eleven years; White-crowned Sparrows, thirteen years; and Song Sparrows, ten years. Even if we assume an average life span of just two to four years for most backyard birds, and this is a realistic estimate, a peek at their reproductive biology should ease our fears about predators' effects on bird populations.

Though some backyard favorites, such as woodpeckers, chickadees, titmice, and nuthatches, nest only once each year, many, including robins, cardinals, bluebirds, towhees, and wrens, raise at least two and sometimes three broods per year. Simple arithmetic suggests that members of a population must only replace themselves over their lifetimes to maintain a stable population. Consequently, any bird needs to reproduce successfully just once in its lifetime to make its contribution to a stable population.

On average, birds do better than this. Some may never rear a brood, but others more than make up the difference. The oldest individuals in a population might ultimately contribute to ten or twelve successful nests in their lifetime. Predators slow the *rate* of population growth, but other factors, such as disease, parasites, weather-related deaths, and accidents, must usually combine with predation to control population size.

In the absence of all these mortality factors, we would be overrun by birds. At first that might not seem such a terrible fate, but too much of anything quickly wears out its welcome. Urban populations of pigeons, House Sparrows, and European Starlings are perfect examples. Reducing predation may be a good idea; eliminating it is not. In predator-proofing nest boxes, 100 percent nest success is not the goal. Our objective as backyard birders should be to reduce predation that results from our failings—poor backyard habitat, poor nest box design, lack of predator deterrents, and poor placement of feeders and nest boxes. If we have done a good job providing for the birds we attract, we should not complain if predators take their fair share. And it might ease your mind just a bit to know that most predators are not nearly as efficient as we think when it comes to taking adult birds. If a hawk makes a kill in one out of four attempts, it is having a good day. When a predator finds a nest, however, it usually consumes the entire contents.

In any case, I often remind myself that reproductive failure is the rule, not the exception, in nature. Among open-nesting songbirds, for example, if 40 percent of the nests in a particular area fledge young—that is, if at least one chick lives long enough to leave the nest—it has been a banner year. A nest success rate of 20 percent—just one in five nests—is more typical. Cavity-nesting birds, on the other hand, are usually more successful. Bluebirds, wrens, and chickadees succeed in fledging young 60 percent of the time.

Regardless of the scientifically recorded rate of nest success, it always seems unfair when predators eat helpless, fragile eggs and chicks. What appears to be a staggering rate of loss, however, rarely influences the overall number of birds. The distressing reports we hear describing declining bird populations usually identify temperate forest fragmentation or tropical habitat destruction as the primary problems.

Occasionally predation can be serious, especially when the prey are uncommon or rare. Each individual of a rare population is proportionately more important than the individuals that make up a larger population. If predators kill fifteen Whooping Cranes when only 150 exist in the wild, for example, we lose 10 percent of the world's population of Whooping Cranes. If, on the other hand, predators kill fifteen robins within a 1-mile radius of my house, I might not even notice. Small population size magnifies the impact of any mortality factor. This is why predator control is often a part of an endangered species recovery plan, but it is not included in efforts to manage more common species.

MAINTAINING AND MONITORING NEST BOXES

Every nest box that has ever housed a family of birds leaves behind a trail rich in natural history. By simply visiting and monitoring nest boxes regularly, landlords can learn ecological lessons firsthand and help improve nest success. Some of these lessons are exhilarating, others are heartbreaking, but all are instructive.

If you've built or bought a suitable nest box, placed it in suitable habitat, and equipped it with a predator guard and/or baffle, it may seem that you have done all you need to do, but you have really just started. Now the fun begins.

Understanding the nesting biology of cavity-nesting birds requires that nest boxes be monitored regularly. Once a week is about right. By visiting nest boxes, you get to observe incubating adults, growing nestlings, and successful fledglings. To ignore an active nest is to miss out on some of nature's most dramatic moments.

Many landlords are reluctant to check active nests—ones that have eggs or chicks in them. That's understandable, because since childhood we've all been bombarded with warnings against disturbing nesting birds. We fear that checking the nest box might cause the birds to abandon the nest. This can happen, but only if the disturbances are frequent and/or they occur during the early stages of incubation. It's OK to periodically check and monitor active bird nests in nest boxes. Just exercise some caution and know what you're doing.

During the egg-laying period, females visit nest boxes early in the morning and lay a single egg each day. This reduces the chances that a predator will see her near the nest and gives her time to feed in anticipation of the commitment she is about to make. So during egg laying, check the nest during the afternoon. Count, study, and even photograph the eggs. Take notes, and show the kids. Stay no longer than one minute, and emphasize to children the importance of adult supervision when checking nests.

Do not disturb the nest while the female incubates the eggs. Incubating females are sensitive to disturbance during the first half of the incubation period and may abandon the nest if disturbed during this time. If you see the female leave the nest box, a quick check is permissible to confirm clutch size. If you open a nest box and find an incubating female warming her eggs, quietly close the nest box and walk away. More often than not she will ignore your intrusion.

After the eggs hatch, which takes about twelve to fourteen days for most small cavity-nesting songbirds, you may again check the nest box every few days without fear of harming the nest. You will know when the eggs hatch, because suddenly one morning both parents will begin bringing food to the nest at two- to five-minute intervals. Watch the nest box, and visit only after you see an adult leave. Again, keep each visit to less than one minute, but feel free to photograph the contents. You can record your observations after you've left the nest box.

Keep a notebook and record the progress of the nest—clutch size, number of eggs that hatch, number of nestlings that fledge. Use your notes to keep track of the age of the nestlings. Most small cavity nesters fledge at sixteen to twenty-one days. By that time, their feathers are well developed, and they can fly well enough to reach the safety of a tree.

When the chicks are about twelve days old, the nest again becomes sensitive to disturbance. As the chicks get older, disturbances excite them, and they sometimes leave the nest before they can fly. Nestlings that leave a nest box prematurely will die. If exposure doesn't get them, predators will. Never disturb a nest after the chicks are twelve days old. This is why it is so important to know the age of the nestlings.

One final word of caution: Open and check nest boxes carefully. Wasps, mice, flying squirrels, and rat snakes sometimes move in. Rodents and snakes may startle you, but most are harmless, although poisonous copperheads have been found in nest boxes in some southern states.

KEEPING A NOTEBOOK

I cannot overstate the importance of recording the observations you make at your nest boxes. Every nest experience is personal and meaningful. After just a few years, you will have accumulated a wealth of experience to draw upon when problems arise. You will find others consulting you for advice. Most important, you will become a better landlord, and your nest boxes will be more successful.

Let me illustrate the value of field notes by sharing just a few months' worth of notes from one particular nest box. The story of nest box HM-4 began in February when I removed a deer mouse nest. (Mice and flying squirrels often occupy nest boxes in the winter.) HM-4 was one of four nest boxes that I hung along a neighbor's fence separating a pasture from the road. Preparing the nest boxes in midwinter allowed them to become a part of the landscape, and thus they were more likely to be used.

I first noticed Eastern Bluebirds investigating HM-4 in early March. As I paralleled the fence on my way to town, I saw a female emerge from the nest box. I stopped the car and watched. Moments later, the male landed on the nest box. Then the female returned and entered the nest box. The male joined her inside. After about a minute, the male emerged and once again perched on the roof of the nest box. He watched as his mate flew to a nearby tree. This curious investigation of the nest box continued for the entire thirty minutes I watched. Clearly the bluebirds were considering HM-4 as a nest site.

A few days later, I noticed a female House Sparrow leave the nest box. I checked, and sure enough, the House Sparrows had already begun building a nest. I removed it. When I returned the next morning, the beginnings of a new House Sparrow nest lined the nest box. Once again, I removed it. For five days we waged this war of wills. I won. The House Sparrows abandoned HM-4, and the very next day the bluebirds returned. For the next week, I saw the bluebirds every time I drove past the nest box. Sometimes they perched on it. Other times they were nearby, hawking insects from a snag or eating rose hips in a multiflora rose thicket. So far, so good. What follows is a diary of events that transpired at HM-4 over the next few weeks.

March 17. HM-4 contains a completed bluebird nest. It is made entirely of dried grasses and fills the nest box almost to the hole. The cup itself is lined with fine grasses; the foundation consists of coarser material. The bluebirds have committed to the nest box.

March 24. No change. The female has not yet laid any eggs.

March 29. Two sky blue eggs rest in the nest. The adults are nowhere to be found.

April 1. As I drive by the nest box, the female leaves, so I stop to check the nest box. Since the female's already gone, I know I'll not disturb her. The nest now contains five eggs, and they are warm to my touch. The clutch is complete, and the fourteen-day incubation period has begun. I note the date so I won't disturb the nest again until just a few days before hatching.

April 4. A spring storm dumps 16 inches of heavy, wet snow on the ridge. I wonder how the bluebirds are faring but resist the temptation to check.

April 11. I approach the nest box quietly on foot, hoping to catch the female on the nest so I can band her. Late in incubation (this is the eleventh of fourteen days), females sit tight. Her investment in the nest has reached a critical stage, and she will flee only if seriously threatened. I place one hand over the hole and slide the other under the door, on top of the incubating female. I grab her firmly and band, weigh, and measure her. The entire process takes less than sixty seconds. Then I put her back on her five eggs, close the door, and hold my hand over the hole for about a minute until she settles down. I walk away, and she remains on the nest as if nothing happened.

April 14. Right on schedule, four tiny hatchlings occupy the nest. The fifth egg is pipped and ready to hatch. Mom sits on the barbed-wire fence and scolds me from just 6 feet away. Dad buzzes my head. I take the hint and leave. Within two minutes of my departure, the female resumes brooding the hatchlings.

April 16. I park the truck about 50 feet from the nest box and watch. About every three minutes, one of the parents visits the nest with a meal for the nestlings. Grubs and fleshy caterpillars seem the foods of choice. In another week, the chicks will be eating grasshoppers and other hard-bodied insects.

April 26. The chicks are now twelve days old and ready to be banded. I fasten a uniquely numbered band to the right leg of each nestling. This will enable me to determine if any of them use one of my nest boxes next year.

April 29. The chicks now fill the nest box. The neat cup is now a flattened mat of grass. Whitewash covers the walls. The nestlings will fledge in a few days, so this will be my last visit to the nest box.

May 2. I notice several speckled juvenile bluebirds in the white oak tree near HM-4. With my binoculars, I can see their bands, and after scanning the branches, I count a total of five. Sweet success!

Having maintained nest box trails in both Oklahoma and West Virginia for nineteen years, my notebooks are filled with dozens of similar anecdotes. Those that come most immediately to mind include several Oklahoma Bewick's Wren nests parasitized by cowbirds, an incubating female chickadee killed by House Sparrows, the American Kestrels that dined regularly on cowbirds and starlings, and the Carolina Chickadees in West Virginia that raised and fledged nine chicks. My favorite remains the pair of Eastern Bluebirds that fledged three broods each year for four consecutive years on a neighbor's West Virginia farm.

After just a few years of carefully observing nest boxes and keeping records, anyone can compile an inventory of similar tales. Then it's off to the local Audubon group or state ornithological society to present a formal paper.

TO CLEAN OR NOT TO CLEAN

For as long as I have studied cavity nesters, the conventional wisdom has been that used nests should be removed as soon as a brood leaves a nest box. Lice, mites, and other parasites that infest old nests lie in wait for any brood that reuses an old nest—or so many references warn. Recent research, however, suggests otherwise.

House Wrens and Purple Martins, for example, show no aversion to using cavities containing old nests. Wayne Davis and two colleagues at the University of Kentucky reported in the *Journal of Field Ornithology* that Eastern Bluebirds actively selected nest boxes containing old nests.

The researchers offered nesting bluebirds paired nest boxes, one empty and one containing an old nest. In thirty-eight of forty-one cases, bluebirds chose the nest box containing the old nest. Other cavity nesters also chose the used nest box in four of five cases. These results suggest that not only might there be no harmful effects, but there may actually be benefits associated with using an old nest.

Davis and his colleagues offer two explanations. Perhaps cavity nesters use old nests simply because it's easier to rebuild a used nest than it is to build a new one. Alternatively, they suggest that bluebirds select old nests because small wasps that parasitize blood-sucking blowfly larvae overwinter in nest boxes. Removing old nests might harm the wasp population, resulting in more blowflies and fewer bluebirds.

If this is the case, we should rethink the practice of removing old nests, at least until a nest box becomes unusable because it's filled with nesting material. Until additional fieldwork confirms this study, perhaps we should adopt a policy of cleaning out every other nest box on a trail. This would ensure a reservoir population of wasps and yet permit half the nest boxes to be freed of all external parasites.

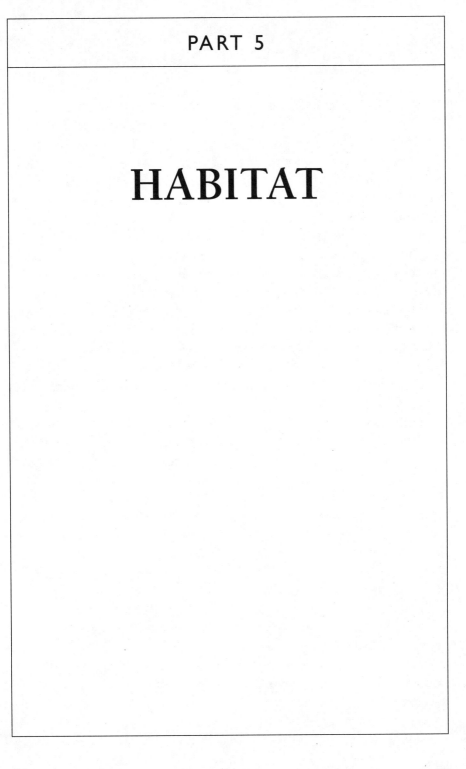

PART 5

HABITAT

ALL-SEASON GARDENING FOR BIRDS

The best long-term way birders can make their property more attractive to birds is to create habitat. This is as true for urban apartment dwellers as it is for country folks who own many acres. The only difference is scale.

In cities, even a rooftop garden or a window box of flowers can attract hummingbirds and small songbirds. Particularly during migration, when cities lie along the shortest distance between two points, a few live plants can be like an oasis in an urban desert to birds on the wing.

Passing hummingbirds might stop to sample nectar from strategically placed bee balms or impatiens. Migrating warblers recognize even small patches of greenery as sources of aphids, spiders, egg cases, caterpillars, flies, and bees. Add a small pool of water with a trickling waterfall, and the oasis is complete. Critical habitat is easy to provide even in the midst of urban sprawl.

The larger and more wild your backyard, the more birds you can expect to visit. Backyards in suburban neighborhoods can attract Mourning Doves, American Robins, Northern Cardinals, Black-capped Chickadees, and even screech-owls. More rural settings can attract virtually any resident bird if suitable food and cover are provided.

Gardening for birds requires plans that extend beyond spring and summer. Though that is when most of the preparation and actual gardening take place, a bird garden pays dividends all year long. More than just a colorful mosaic of backyard vegetation, it offers sanctuary from predators, protection from the elements, and natural food.

In late spring and early summer, flowers provide nectar for hummingbirds and shrubs provide nesting sites for everything from Gray Catbirds and Northern Mockingbirds to Chipping Sparrows and Brown Thrashers. By late summer and early fall, fruit-bearing trees, shrubs, and vines reward robins, bluebirds, waxwings, tanagers, and other fruit eaters. Throughout the winter and early spring, evergreens such as pines and spruces provide essential cover for roosting birds. And every day, dense backyard plantings provide safe haven from predators.

To maximize the value of any bird garden, you must understand the ecological needs of the birds you hope to attract. In the Northeast, for example, that means planting nectar-producing flowers that bloom May through September for hummingbirds. In southern California, on the other hand, Anna's Hummingbirds are very active in December and begin nesting in January.

Though establishing a garden of any sort is usually done in the spring, anxious northern birders can get a jump on spring by starting seedlings or plants indoors in a greenhouse or outdoors in a cold frame. By the time warm spring temperatures and rain arrive, plants are already off to a vigorous head start.

The best plants for bird gardens vary geographically. What's effective in New York will be quite different from what might be prescribed for New Mexico. A list of specific wildflowers, shrubs, and vines for every region of the country is beyond the scope of this book. Look for a reputable local garden center or nursery that carries native perennial wildflowers, shrubs, and vines. Get to know the staff, find someone who knows both plants and birds, and ask questions. Plants that are naturally adapted and acclimated to your part of the country will do much better in your backyard than exotics or ornamentals raised elsewhere.

A bird garden is a great way to get children interested in both birds and conservation. Show kids the results of dirty hands, and you will help nurture a new generation of birders and conservationists. They will learn from experience the critical interrelationship between birds and habitat. It is hands-on lessons like these that last a lifetime.

RAISING SUNFLOWERS AND GRAINS FOR BIRDS

Raising sunflowers and grains is simple, inexpensive, and a great way to reduce your bird food budget. All you need is a small patch of fertile ground that receives full sunlight and water for irrigation, if necessary. Simply devote a portion of the backyard or even an existing garden to birdseed production. If you are cursed with poor soil, fill a few raised beds with topsoil.

The obvious choices for a bird food garden are sunflowers—black striped, gray striped, black oil, and white oil. They thrive in full sun, and even just a few heads yield a surprising amount of seed. Though seeds from packaged bird food can be used to sow a new crop, fresh seed from a garden center usually produces larger, more vigorous plants. To maximize production in a small space, try the Mammoth Russian variety. The flower heads are huge and can yield hundreds, even thousands of seeds.

Follow planting directions on the package, and by next fall your crop will be ready to harvest. Finches, cardinals, chickadees, and other sunflower lovers will flock to the standing crop, or you can cut the ripe heads and hang them in the garage for later use.

White, golden, and red millets appeal to many native sparrows, finches, doves, and cardinals, so if space permits, you might want to cultivate a millet patch. Once again, birds can be permitted to eat the standing crop, or you can cut, hang, and dry it for later use.

In the southwestern states, milo can also be grown in a backyard setting. Though milo is considered an undesirable filler seed in most parts of the country, results from the Cornell University Laboratory of Ornithology's Project Feederwatch survey indicate that some southwestern species eat milo regularly. Inca Doves, Stellar's Jays, Curve-billed Thrashers, Gambel's Quail, and a variety of native sparrows are among the species that choose milo when given a choice among several seeds.

Corn is also easily grown in gardens, though most of us consider it an ephemeral late-summer dinner treat. Allocate some corn for birds, however, and its rewards can extend well into winter. Wild Turkeys, Ring-necked Pheasants, quail, crows, doves, jays, and Red-bellied and Red-headed Woodpeckers head the list of birds that enjoy whole corn kernels.

The last group of seeds that can be homegrown is often overlooked because we grow these plants for their fruits and typically throw the seeds away. Watermelon, cantaloupe, pumpkins, and squashes are filled with seeds that many desirable birds love. Rather than toss these seeds when eating the fruits, save them for the birds. Just rinse the seeds, and dry them on a sheet of butcher paper. Then store them in a container as you would any other seed. Cardinals, chickadees, titmice, nuthatches, and woodpeckers relish these seeds, and some seed packagers are even putting them in some of their better mixes.

WILDFLOWERS FOR BIRDS

When the conversation turns to wildflowers and birds, most birders think hummingbirds—with good reason. Hummingbirds visit backyard wildflower gardens all across the continent. No matter where you live, there are at least a few species of tubular, nectar-bearing flowers that hummers count among their favorites.

Wildflowers, however, produce more than just nectar. In some cases, mature seed heads attract a variety of finches and other seedeaters. If we extend the definition just a bit, we can add grasses and their seeds to the list. Many native sparrows subsist on grass seeds during certain times of year. Even hard-to-attract fruit-eating birds can be coaxed into a backyard landscaped with wildflowers that produce succulent berries.

Among the easiest food-producing wildflowers to grow are members of the sunflower family, which attract flocks of goldfinches, siskins, and other finches. Smaller members of the sunflower family also produce abundant seed crops and brighten backyard wildflower beds. Daisies, asters, zinnias, marigolds, and thistles come in a variety of colors and by late summer feed a variety of birds. In August and September goldfinches in my backyard spend as much time on these plants as they do at my feeders. Even the weediest members of this group—the goldenrods, ragweeds, and dandelions—feed many species of finches and sparrows. In the spring and early summer, finches congregate on the dandelion heads interspersed among the grasses; in the fall, they gather in a nearby field where the goldenrod is more plentiful than dirt.

Pokeweed and blackberries are hard to beat for attracting bluebirds, waxwings, robins, catbirds, and mockingbirds. Pokeweed grows as an annual in the North but thrives as a perennial in the South. It prefers moist, fertile soils and often grow profusely as a roadside weed. My pokeweed patch is all volunteer and always the site of intense activity in September when the plump berries ripen and turn deep purplish black. In addition to the fruit eaters listed above, I've seen woodpeckers, cardinals, Scarlet Tanagers, and Brown Thrashers in the pokeweed patch.

In a backyard setting, blackberries provide three valuable functions: Their white flowers brighten the backyard in the spring; their dense growth provides protective nesting cover for cardinals, buntings, towhees, catbirds, and native sparrows; and fruit eaters find their berries irresistible. My wife also loves blackberries, so every year we compete with the birds to harvest the plumpest, juiciest fruits. Usually we get the seconds.

TREES FOR BIRDS

If you want to enjoy backyard birds for the next twenty or thirty years, consider planting a few trees each year. Properly chosen, trees bear fruit and nuts and provide nest sites, escape cover, and song perches. The major drawback is that most trees grow slowly and take years to become most attractive to birds. Once established, however, a stand of trees becomes a hub for back-yard bird life.

The best way to get trees started is to buy older, mature trees at a rep-utable garden center or nursery. Expect to pay $50 to $500 for large, estab-lished trees. The payoff is that older transplanted trees yield food and dense cover years, if not decades, before trees planted as seedlings.

Consider trees as an investment in the future. They not only provide food and cover for birds, they also improve the appearance of the property, make homes more energy efficient, and increase the resale value of the property. Deciduous trees planted on the south side of a house shade the building dur-ing the summer and help keep it cool; in the winter, after the leaves have fallen, sunshine helps warm the house. A bank of conifers on the west or north side of a house protects the building from chilling prevailing winds. When all the benefits of trees are considered, it is easier to justify their expense.

When deciding which trees to plant, the possibilities can seem over-whelming. The best choices vary from region to region. A few suggestions are offered here to get you started, then consult a good garden center for more specific tips and recommendations.

Some of the best trees to cultivate in any part of the continent are oaks. Acorns are a favorite food of everything from gamebirds and woodpeckers to jays and nuthatches. In the Northeast, white, red, and black oaks are good choices. In the South and along the Pacific coast, plant live oaks. In the prairie states, post, blackjack, and burr oaks do well. And in western mountains and valleys, try Gambel's oak.

Virtually any nut- or fruit-bearing tree makes a terrific addition to a back-yard bird sanctuary. Pecan, walnut, and beech trees attract the same species that enjoy acorns. Mulberries, cherries, plums, crab apples, and figs draw waxwings, bluebirds, robins, mockingbirds, catbirds, thrashers, and tanagers.

Conifers offer year-round cover and should be a part of every backyard habitat. Chipping and Lark Sparrows, doves, jays, mockingbirds, and robins nest in pines and spruces during the breeding season; during the winter, many species roost amid the protective cover of evergreen branches. Many finches also extract the seeds from the cones of pine, fir, and spruce trees for food.

SHRUBS AND HEDGES FOR BIRDS

Cardinals, catbirds, thrashers, mockingbirds, buntings, various warblers, and many native sparrows share an important habitat requirement that every backyard birder should know: They all nest in shrubs. Most of them also eat the fruits and berries that these shrubs produce each summer and fall. When the shrubs bloom, they attract a variety of pollinators, including colorful butterflies and hummingbirds. Even flowers that yield little nectar attract hummers, which glean aphids, spiders, gnats, and other small, soft-bodied invertebrates from flowers of all sorts. Of all the vegetation we might plant in our backyards, birds will probably find shrubs the most irresistible.

What shrubs you should plant is determined by where you live. Visit a garden center or nursery for advice on which species do best in your area. When planting shrubs, however, worry more about growth form than species. You want shrubs that grow into dense thickets to provide nesting and escape cover. Thorny species are better than thornless species. Dense, thorny shrubs offer safe haven from hawks, owls, cats, and other predators. Roses, blackberries, gooseberries, and hawthorns are ideal.

Shop for shrubs that are several years old so they will not take years to mature. Then plant them in the fall. Four to six months of winter dormancy allows plants to acclimate to local conditions. When spring arrives, fall-planted shrubs usually grow quickly and vigorously. Spring-planted shrubs often experience transplant shock and grow slowly the first year.

No backyard bird garden is complete without a few fruit-bearing shrubs to provide food and cover. A long hedge, perhaps along a property line, is even better. If you doubt this advice, you have never seen a flock of waxwings, robins, or bluebirds descend on the shrubs in your backyard.

ATTRACTING BIRDS WITH SUCCULENTS

If you live in the Southwest and your attempts to attract birds with plants have been stymied by heat and drought, give succulents a try. Succulents are drought-resistant plants that have thick-skinned, fleshy leaves and/or stems. These adaptations reduce water loss to evaporation and transpiration by limiting the surface area exposed to the air. Furthermore, their fleshy nature allows succulents to store water, which enables them to survive periods of extended drought. Many also have shallow root systems to take advantage of the short-lived surface water that falls during seasonal thunderstorms and cloudbursts. This combination of characteristics makes succulents ideal garden plants anywhere rainfall is limited and summer temperatures soar.

Cacti and yuccas are among the most familiar succulents, and many provide food and cover for a variety of birds. Many succulents also produce showy flowers, so their value includes aesthetic as well as ornithological appeal.

Succulents require well-drained soil. If their roots get wet for extended periods, they rot, and the plants die. Water sparingly, and let the soil dry thoroughly between waterings. If your soil is inadequate, or if you decide to pot your succulents so you can move them around the backyard, create succulent soil by blending one part coarse washed builder's sand with one part roughly screened compost. A cup of bone meal for every bushel of soil makes the soil even better. For more details on cultivation and maintenance, consult a local nursery or garden center.

Among the easiest succulents to grow and among the most attractive to birds is prickly pear (*Opuntia* spp.). It typically grows as a low, herbaceous plant characterized by jointed stems and spiny pads. The flowers are often quite bright and showy, and the fruits and seeds are eaten by doves, quail, roadrunners, turkeys, ravens, thrashers, woodpeckers, and Cactus Wrens. Equally important, the thorny cover provided by the prickly pads provides excellent nest sites for doves, thrashers, roadrunners, Cactus Wrens, and a variety of native sparrows.

For the southwestern counterpart of the easterner who plants acorns to grow oak trees, saguaro cactus is a long-lived giant that provides a favorite nest site for Gila Woodpeckers and Gilded Flickers. Abandoned woodpecker holes are subsequently used by small owls, kestrels, Brown-crested Flycatchers, Cactus Wrens, and Purple Martins. Ash-throated Flycatchers and flickers eat saguaro flowers, and Gila Woodpeckers, Curve-billed Thrashers, doves, Cactus Wrens, and flickers eat the fruits. Saguaro populations have been declining for years, so it is illegal to transplant saguaros from the wild, but they are available at reputable cactus nurseries. If you are patient and have a few decades to nurse a saguaro (they grow less than 2 inches per year and live for up to 200 years), it makes an excellent addition to a desert backyard.

Yuccas (*Yucca* spp.) appeal to a variety of birds and are widely distributed. Members of the lily family, yuccas grow commonly throughout the Southwest, but many species are surprisingly hardy. I have several in my backyard in northern West Virginia, and I have read that, if protected from prevailing winter winds, some species grow as far north as Minnesota and New York. Verdins, doves, and House Finches nest among the yucca's dense spear-shaped leaves, and orioles and hummingbirds sip nectar from yucca flowers.

Xerophytic gardening—using drought-tolerant plants—is becoming increasingly popular all across America, if only because it conserves precious water. In the East, Americans apply 30 percent of municipal water to their lawns. In the West, the proportion jumps to 60 percent. Succulent gardening is an ecologically correct first step to more natural, low-water lawn care. That it can attract birds is our good fortune.

ATTRACTING HUMMINGBIRDS

Amid a perfectly manicured bed of brightly colored flowers, a brilliant flash of sparkling ruby red caught my eye. I watched the creature zip from flower to flower, pausing just a moment or two at each one before moving on to the next. After several minutes, it disappeared down an embankment.

I was ten years old, and that was how I saw my first hummingbird. It was a Ruby-throat in Pennsylvania. I saw it while delivering newspapers one day in late May. At the time, though, I didn't know what it was. Its wings beat so fast they blurred. I thought it might be an insect. I had read of hummingbirds, but I never imagined I might see one in a neighbor's backyard.

When the last newspaper was delivered, I raced home on my bike and pulled out my dog-eared Golden Guides to insects and birds. It was the most incredible creature I'd ever seen—a hummingbird!

Years later, I found a hummingbird nest. It held two tiny, bean-size eggs and an incubating female that could rise off the nest like a helicopter.

Those two observations hooked me on birds, and I suspect many experienced bird-watchers could tell similar stories. Who could discover such a tiny, colorful, and energetic creature and not want to see it again and again? Hummingbirds truly are some of nature's jewels.

Fortunately for those hooked on hummers, they are relatively easy to attract to backyards. Along the southern tier of states, some species can be seen all year long. Farther north, hummers brighten our gardens and lives from April through October.

PROVIDING FOOD

The simplest way to attract hummers is to hang a nectar feeder in suitable habitat. For most species, that means a wooded area, thicket, or forest edge with a waterway nearby. Without at least some appropriate habitat, hoping for hummers can be an exercise in futility. Residents of recent suburban developments are often frustrated by the absence of hummers. Poor habitat is usually the reason.

For those lucky enough to live near suitable habitat, attracting hummingbirds can be surprisingly easy. Nectar feeders are designed to simulate nectar-bearing flowers. They are usually bright red because most hummingbirds find red more attractive than other colors. Just fill the feeder with a solution of one part table sugar to four parts water, and you're in business.

There are, however, some other points to keep in mind. When mixing nectar, use boiling water. This helps the mixture stay fresh longer. And be sure to add the sugar to the boiled water; don't boil the mixture. This can cause some of the water to evaporate and concentrate the nectar. If nectar is too sweet, it can damage a bird's liver; if it's not sweet enough, hummers may ignore it. So be sure to use the one part sugar to four parts water recipe. This approximates the sweetness of nectar in nature.

FEEDERS

Nectar feeders can be found in wild bird stores, garden centers, and other retailers that cater to outdoor enthusiasts. Most work well, but I prefer those that are easiest to clean. Typically these are saucer-style feeders. They are covered with a lid with several feeding ports. The lid lifts completely off for easy cleaning. This is important, because during warm weather, nectar feeders can get slimy and moldy. My favorite nectar feeders are the HummZinger Excel and Nectar Bar by Aspects, Inc.

It's best to clean nectar feeders at least every other day with detergent and/or a 10 percent bleach solution. Just be sure to rinse the feeders thoroughly before refilling with nectar. Bottle feeders are more difficult to clean and usually require the use of a brush.

Another consideration is whether the feeder should be glass or plastic. Glass breaks when dropped, so I prefer high-tech clear, hard, plastic feeders.

FEEDER PLACEMENT

A frequent question, especially from new hummingbird watchers, is where to place a nectar feeder. Hanging it from a step-in pole in a flower bed or a hook on the porch or deck is ideal. Nearby hanging plants can make porch or deck feeders particularly attractive. If you have never fed hummers before, tie an 18- to 24-inch-long length of red ribbon to the feeder. The ribbon blowing in the breeze makes a new feeder easier for birds to spot.

If you hang just a single feeder and there are more than a few hummers in the neighborhood, you will quickly discover how aggressive and territorial these little birds can be. Dominant individuals sometimes claim a feeder and drive other birds away. One solution is to add more feeders. Either hang feeders on each side of the house, each out of eyeshot of the other, or bunch them together so no one individual can possibly defend them all.

Western watchers familiar with Rufous Hummingbirds know that they are extremely aggressive when defending a food source. In *Hummingbirds of North America* (University of New Mexico Press, 1994), Dan True suggested an ingenious solution to the Rufous's aggression. Among the Rufous Hummingbird's favorite sources of nectar is the century plant, whose nectar-rich flowers grow 8 to 15 feet above the ground. To capitalize on this, True placed one feeder 12 feet high on one side of his house, and he made the nectar just a bit sweeter than usual. He then placed several feeders less than 3 feet high and several more 5 or 6 feet above the ground. The Rufous claimed and defended the sweeter, elevated feeder and ignored the others. Tiny Calliope Hummingbirds, which typically feed on low-growing flowers, used the low feeders. The Black-chins and Broad-tails shared the feeders at the intermediate height. By providing nectar at three different heights, True reduced aggression among the four species that visited his backyard. It's reassuring to know that a thoughtful human can outwit birds that weigh less than a quarter.

DEALING WITH ANTS AND BEES

One problem that many hummingbird watchers eventually encounter is how to deal with the ants, bees, and wasps that find nectar as irresistible as hummers do. Ant guards are effective and readily available. An ant guard is simply a small, moatlike container suspended between the feeder and its hanger. Fill the moat with soapy water or salad oil, and ants become trapped when they try to cross the barrier. Many nectar feeders are now manufactured with built-in ant guards. Look for this feature on the packaging.

Bees and wasps can be discouraged on some feeders by installing bee guards. These small, plastic grids fit over the ports and make it difficult for insects to reach the nectar. And again, some manufacturers have redesigned their ports to make it difficult for bees and wasps to sip nectar.

Another option is to paint the edges of drinking ports with Avon's Skin-So-Soft. It's an effective insect repellent. Just be sure to keep the Skin-So-Soft from dripping into the nectar.

GARDENING FOR HUMMINGBIRDS

If providing nectar feeders is the quickest and simplest way to attract hummingbirds to a backyard, planting nectar-bearing flowers is the best long-term approach. With a little thought and planning, anyone can design a backyard that is both pleasing to the eye and irresistible to hummingbirds.

The first step is to draw a rough sketch of the backyard; include all existing trees, shrubs, and wildflowers. Place the hummingbird garden where you will get the most enjoyment from it. That might be outside a large living room window or off the deck or back porch. Then plant a few species of nectar-bearing wildflowers. Plant smaller species in front, between the viewing area and the back of the garden, so you always have a full view of the flowers. And talk to experts at a local garden center for help in selecting species that will bloom over a period of months. You don't want everything blooming at the same time. Local experts can also recommend which species grow best in your area. Here are some general guidelines.

In California, try clematis, flowering quince, red sages, butterfly bush, honeysuckle, and mimosa. In the Pacific Northwest, start with impatiens, Indian paintbrush, phlox, fuchsia, and currants. In the Southwest, plant red sages, century plants, ocotillo, lantana, and Mexican honeysuckle. In the western mountains, try currants, butterfly bush, red penstemons, sages, bee balm, blazing star, and skyrocket. In the Southeast, go with trumpet creeper, flowering quince, mimosa, lantana, salvias, and azaleas. And in the Northeast and Midwest, start with bee balm, cardinal flower, hollyhock, flowering crab apple, impatiens, and red buckeye.

When planning a hummingbird garden, keep in mind that it is a long-term project. Unless you buy mature plants at a nursery or garden center, perennials take several years to bloom. Once established, however, they provide years of relatively maintenance-free enjoyment. One way to jump-start a nectar garden is to plant annuals along with perennials. They live just one year but usually bloom profusely. Even species such as zinnias, which are not great nectar producers, attract hummingbirds—they eat the spiders, aphids, gnats, and other tiny invertebrates that inevitably inhabit fresh flowers.

A less obvious, though important, component of any hummingbird garden is water. Hummers easily meet their water needs from the nectar they drink, but they love to bathe. They particularly enjoy soaking themselves in a fine mist on hot summer days. Install a mister among the leaves of a tree or shrub near your feeders. Misters can be adjusted so they use very little water.

Creating a hummingbird garden takes time, patience, and planning. Start small, with just a few species. Each year, experiment and add a few more. Not everything will thrive, and you'll learn as you go.

HUMMINGBIRDS

Hummingbirds inhabit most of North America. Twenty-six species have been confirmed in the United States and Canada, though only fourteen nest here regularly. The East has a single species: the Ruby-throated Hummingbird, which commonly nests east of a line that bisects the Great Plains.

The Broad-tailed Hummingbird occurs widely throughout the western mountains. If you ever hike the Rocky Mountains, you're likely to encounter a Broad-tail. Listen for the male's cricketlike wing buzz. The Calliope Hummingbird also inhabits the western mountains, though its range is more northwest than the Broad-tail's. Look for Calliopes feeding low to the ground in mountain meadows. The Black-chinned Hummingbird occurs widely in the West, from west Texas to southern California and north into British Columbia.

The Rufous Hummingbird breeds in the Pacific Northwest all the way north to Alaska. It ranges widely during migration and has been seen in forty-seven different states, including Michigan, Pennsylvania, Massachusetts, and Ontario.

The Buff-bellied Hummingbird nests from the lower Rio Grande Valley of Texas to Mexico's Yucatan Peninsula. During the nonbreeding season, Buff-bellies can be found along the Gulf coast all the way to the Florida panhandle.

Allen's Hummingbird occurs along the coast of California south into Baja and the Mexican mainland. Anna's and Costa's Hummingbirds also occur in California. Their range extends eastward into Arizona.

The mother lode of U.S. hummingbird distribution is found in southeastern Arizona. There you can find Beryline, Blue-throated, Broad-billed, Lucifer, Magnificent, Violet-crowned, and White-eared Hummingbirds. It wouldn't be unreasonable to see all these species in hummingbird meccas such as Ramsey and Madera Canyons. The range of the Magnificent Hummingbird extends into New Mexico, and that of the Lucifer Hummingbird extends eastward to west Texas.

FALL GARDENING

Mention gardening, and most people think spring. I do. But experience has taught me that the best time to garden for birds, butterflies, and other wildlife is the fall. By getting perennial wildflowers, shrubs, vines, and even trees in the ground in October or November, plants have time to acclimate to the soil and climate before the onset of winter dormancy. Come spring, acclimated plants grow vigorously and often outperform specimens planted in the spring. Being in the ground for six to eight months gives fall plantings an invaluable head start.

Fall gardening is also considerably less expensive than traditional spring plantings. Garden centers and nurseries do most of their business in the spring because that's when most folks do their gardening. Demand allows retailers to raise prices and maximize profits. By waiting until late summer or early fall, those of us who garden for wildlife can save a lot of money by taking advantage of end-of-season sales. Rather than throw out leftovers, retailers slash prices to empty the store. If you purchase several dozen plants, this buying strategy can save hundreds of dollars.

There is, however, a downside to fall gardening. By August and September many retailers have sold out of their most popular plants. Fortunately, "wild" gardeners often prefer plants that more traditional gardeners eschew. Shop carefully, and bargains can be found.

The obvious places to shop for native plants are nurseries and garden centers. (Mail-order outlets usually limit their business to spring sales.) Find a retailer with a knowledgeable staff, and reward it with your business. Another great source for native plants is local nature centers. In Pittsburgh, for example, the Audubon Society of Western Pennsylvania began propagating wildflowers from seed several years ago and now has a popular annual sale. And in eastern Pennsylvania, Bowman's Hill Wildflower Preserve near New Hope sells native wildflower seeds and has an annual sale of mature plants. With homeowner interest in native plants exploding nationwide, I suspect many nature centers offer similar opportunities.

The joys of a colorful wild garden are many. Fragrant wildflowers grace the dinner table May through September. Hummingbirds vie for rights to precious supplies of nectar. Robins, bluebirds, and waxwings mob the berry patch. And goldfinches, towhees, and cardinals parade in and out of the sunflowers on the far end of the vegetable garden.

Among the first questions any new "wild" gardener asks is "Should I plant seeds or buy mature plants?" The answer depends on your budget and time frame. Though wildflower seeds are expensive, they are still usually cheaper than mature plants. But seeds may take years to develop into mature plants. Perennial wildflowers usually take at least three years to bloom. Shrubs and vines can take three to eight years to mature, and trees take even longer.

One way to reduce the expense of wildflower seeds is to collect them in late summer and fall. Hikes along quiet country roads are often fruitful. Better yet, get landowner permission to collect seeds in old fields and along forest edges. Many farmers will be grateful for your help in controlling undesirable "weeds."

I prefer more immediate results, so I buy mature plants. I budget $200 to $300 per year for wildflowers and shrubs. The first few years, progress was slow, but at least I had some blooms and berries immediately. Now that I've been at it for over a decade, the cumulative effect is amazing. My backyard is ringed with nectar-, seed-, and fruit-bearing plants. The focal point of the front yard is a perennial garden that measures 8 by 12 feet. During the summer, visitors often remark on the steady stream of hummingbirds and butterflies that visit my small collection of bee balm, purple coneflower, butterfly milkweed, black-eyed Susans, Indian blanket, and daisies.

As your plantings spread, you can reduce your annual expenses by thinning and transplanting your own plants. Generous friends and neighbors are often happy to share their plants, too. Another huge advantage to transplanting your own flowers and shrubs is that they are preadapted to local environmental conditions—soil type, rainfall, temperature—so their chances for survival are excellent.

Transplanting flowers and shrubs, whether purchased at a nursery or relocated from your own backyard, is simple. Dig a hole slightly larger than the root ball being transplanted. Wet the hole thoroughly, then place the transplant into the hole. Fill the hole with rich soil, and tamp it firmly. Be sure to include some of the original soil you removed from the hole, because it may contain some symbiotic fungi that promote vigorous plant growth. Water the new plant regularly to keep its roots damp until late fall or the first hard freeze. Then protect the plant with a layer of mulch until spring.

When planning a wild garden, consider function, phenology, structure, and aesthetics. Every plant in a wild garden should have a purpose. Nectar-bearing, tubular flowers attract hummingbirds. Seed-bearing composites, members of the sunflower family, feed finches and other seedeaters. Blackberries, raspberries, roses, grapes, mulberries, and other fruit-bearing shrubs and trees attract bluebirds, robins, catbirds, tanagers, mockingbirds, thrashers, and waxwings. And trees and shrubs with dense growth forms, such as blackberries and hawthorns, provide secure nesting sites for native sparrows, buntings, cardinals, and towhees.

Phenology is the branch of biology that covers predictable, seasonal phenomena. Bird migration and fall leaf drops are classic phenological events. Plan wildflower gardens with natural plant phenology in mind. By allowing spring blooms to give way to summer blossoms and fall flowers, backyards can be colorful from April to October. Ask the professionals at a local garden center for advice on which plants bloom when.

Another concern is the eventual size of the mature plant. Bee balm, a hummingbird favorite in the East, and joe-pye weed, a popular late-summer butterfly plant, can grow quite tall, so they should be planted at the rear of any small bed, or they'll disrupt your view of smaller species. And give plants room to grow. A good rule of thumb is to allow each wildflower about 1 square foot of space. When first planted, a garden may appear sparsely populated, but by the end of the second growing season, it will have bushed out nicely. By the third or fourth season, many species will be ready to split and transplant.

Trees and larger shrubs pose a more difficult planning problem; it's easy to underestimate their eventual size. When I transplanted a flowering dogwood from the woods to a spot just off the corner of the deck, it was a perfect fit. A few years later, the tree was 10 feet tall and obstructed my view of one of my busier feeding stations. Next time, I'll know better. Visualize potential problems before planting trees or shrubs that might someday obstruct important sight lines.

Finally, any wild garden should be as appealing to the gardener as it is to the birds and butterflies. A backyard can be a canvas for a palette of natural colors—snow white daisies, scarlet bee balm, yellow brown-eyed Susans, blue sage, and purple coneflowers. Wild gardening is a great way to blend a love of nature with an artistic eye.

If a wild garden sounds like a good idea for your backyard, start in the fall so your garden gets a head start in the spring. Begin with a sketch of the backyard. Mark the location of the house, deck, patio, driveway, and all existing trees and shrubs. Then indicate the areas where you would like to add color, nectar, seeds, fruits, and cover. I suggest you start small. Gardening can be hard work. If you buy too many plants at first, a wonderful project can quickly become a horrendous chore. It's better to make several visits to the garden center, as time and money permit, than to try to create a wild garden in a single day.

WINTER HABITAT

Every morning at daybreak from Thanksgiving until Easter, scores of birds emerge from a thorny tangle of briers and vines on the edge of the woods near my house. Cardinals, juncos, goldfinches, and a variety of native sparrows sleep in the thicket at night during cold, inclement weather. The nearly impenetrable growth hides the birds from predators and protects them from wind, snow, and rain. More than once I've seen Sharp-shinned Hawks stymied by the brambles, and after a snowstorm, the thicket seems like an igloo for birds. Dense vegetation is an essential habitat component that helps winter residents make it through the winter.

Habitat comes in several forms—food, water, and cover—but it is cover that is critical during the short days and long nights of winter. Providing valuable escape cover and shelter from the elements can be either a short-term or long-term project.

BRUSH PILES

For immediate results, build a brush pile. Collect large branches that you have trimmed from your trees or gather them from neighbors. Lay them crosswise, in tic-tac-toe fashion, in a corner of the yard. Add to it each year until it meets your needs. Try to build a 6-by-6-foot brush pile at least 3 feet tall the first year. A brush pile can be made almost weatherproof by inserting an old piece of plywood about 3 feet above the ground.

Another source of brush pile material is used Christmas trees. I collect neighbors' Christmas trees every January, and retailers often give me ones that remain unsold. They add a welcome splash of color to an otherwise drab brush pile. Used Christmas trees can also be placed under a bird feeder. Tie the tree down so it doesn't blow all over the yard on windy days, or tie several together. Old Christmas trees provide ground-feeding birds with protective cover from snow and wind and a safe haven from bird-eating hawks and cats.

PLANTING WINTER COVER

A more long-term solution to the winter habitat problem is to plant dense stands of trees and shrubs. Conifers are an excellent choice. Various species of pines, spruces, firs, and cedars are native to all parts of the country. All provide excellent winter cover, and robins, doves, and jays are just a few of the birds that nest in conifers.

If you're new to the birdscaping business, get to know the most knowledgeable employees at a local nursery. Ask questions. Make sure the plants you buy are locally grown so they are adapted to your area's environmental conditions. Buy plants that are mature. Shrubs should be 3 or 4 feet tall, and the stems should be at least 1 inch in diameter. Trees should be at least 5 feet tall and have a large root ball. Smaller, less mature plants are readily available (especially by mail order) and less expensive, but they take years to produce usable cover. Reputable nurseries grow their own stock and guarantee their plants; usually they will replace at no charge any plants that die during the first year.

Another way to provide winter cover is to plant dense deciduous thickets. Roses, raspberries, blackberries, barberries, and honeysuckles grow in dense tangles and provide excellent winter roosting habitat as well as escape cover. Hawks, owls, foxes, and other mammalian predators usually give up the chase when a potential victim flies into a dense thicket. These shrubs also produce succulent fruits that many birds feast on from midsummer through fall.

To make thickets even more protective, plant a few trumpetcreeper, grape, or Virginia creeper vines nearby and allow them to crawl through the thicket. In just a few years, you'll have an impenetrable tangle that only birds can use.

ROOST BOXES

Though many songbirds roost in dense vegetation, some cavity nesters prefer to sleep in tree cavities or even nest boxes on cold winter nights. Bluebirds, Winter Wrens, and White-breasted and Pygmy Nuthatches roost communally on frigid nights. Ten or more individuals sometimes cram into a cavity. By sharing body heat in a small space, these birds can make it through winter's cruelest weather.

A bird-friendly backyard should include accommodations for cavity-roosting birds. That could include allowing a large, hole-riddled dead tree to stand or keeping nesting boxes up and open all year long. Another option is to provide a roost box. A roost box is larger than a normal nest box, is tightly sealed except for the entrance at the bottom (to conserve rising body heat), and has a series of staggered dowel rod perches from the bottom to the top of the box. The idea is to maximize the number of birds that can comfortably fit into the box and to conserve body heat and minimize heat loss.

A roost box measures approximately 10 inches square and 24 inches high. There should be no air vents, and all upper joints can be sealed with a silicone bead to completely eliminate air flow. The only opening is a $2^1/2$-inch entrance hole cut into the bottom of the front panel. Inside, a series of $1/4$-inch dowels runs from side to side. The dowels should be staggered to minimize the amount of droppings that fall from birds perched above onto those perched below. Finally, be sure one side or the bottom of the box is removable so it can be cleaned out occasionally. Hang the roost box 5 to 8 feet above the ground in an open southerly exposure to take advantage of solar radiation, and if possible, place it so it is protected from the prevailing winds.

PART 6

ENJOYING BIRDS MORE

HOW TO
IDENTIFY UNFAMILIAR BIRDS

Y ou see a bird you have never seen before. It may be at a feeder in the backyard, at a nearby park, or in a South American rain forest. You are a birder, so you want to attach a name to it. The bird may fly at any moment, never to be seen again, and there is no one nearby to tell you what it is. You are alone. How do you identify this potential life bird?

Too often birders, both seasoned veterans and beginners, take a quick look to get an overall impression of the bird, then dive immediately into a field guide. Often they are disappointed because when they realize they have missed a critical field mark, the bird is gone.

It makes more sense to use a step-by-step technique to identify birds, especially when you are alone. The first step is to study the bird as long as it presents itself. Do not take your eyes off it. Note key field marks. Whether you see the bird for two seconds or two minutes, take advantage of every moment to gather information. Put down your binoculars only after the bird leaves.

The next step is to grab your notebook and write down everything you can remember about the bird. Do this immediately. Waiting a few minutes or hours is a big mistake. Your memory of a collection of fine details fades surprisingly fast. Only after you have written a complete description of the bird should you refer to your trusty field guide.

THE IMPORTANCE OF LOOKING CLOSELY

The most obvious characteristic, and probably the first to zero in on, is a bird's **size.** Field guides include measurements of birds, but it is tough to determine whether a bird is 5 inches or 7 inches long when seen through binoculars at 30 yards. Rather than attempt to guess actual size, compare the new bird to known standards. Is it small like a chickadee, medium like a robin, or large like a crow? Determining the general size immediately rules out hundreds of possibilities.

After size, focus on **shapes.** The head may be flat, round, or crested. The bill may be long, short, heavy, or dainty. It may be spearlike, chisel-like, compressed, depressed, decurved, recurved, hooked, or crossed. Wings may be narrow and pointed, broad and round, concave or flat. The neck and legs may be notably long or short. The tail may be square, rounded, notched, or forked. Sometimes a characteristic shape is all you need to identify a bird. When I made my first cross-country trip in August, 1974, I stopped at a rest area on I-40 in western Oklahoma. I saw a trim, medium-size bird perched on the power lines. It had a deeply forked, scissor-shaped tail. Even as a novice birder, I knew it was a Scissor-tailed Flycatcher. Some birds, on the other hand, have no distinctive shapes. They simply look like generic songbirds. The absence of distinctive characteristics can be as important as their presence.

Another obvious field mark on many birds is **color.** In fact, color is so obvious it can be distracting. We can get so caught up in a bird's beauty that we forget the urgency of observing other field marks. The bird may fly away at any moment. Assume it will. Stay focused and note each in the series of field marks quickly, thoroughly, and methodically.

The location of colors is just as important as their presence. A small bird with a blue head, red body, and green back is a Painted Bunting. A blue bird that's larger than a chickadee and smaller than a robin and has a wide chestnut wing bar is a Blue Grosbeak. A huge pink bird with an orange tail and a long, flat bill is a Roseate Spoonbill.

Colors can also be tricky, especially in bright sunlight. At certain angles, yellow becomes orange, red appears yellow, and brown turns red. Beware when watching brightly lit birds. One summer I had a chance to observe Black Guillemots at close range from a blind on Eastern Egg Rock in Maine. I discovered that up close and in bright light, Black Guillemots are, in fact, dark iridescent green.

Sometimes the absence of color is notable. Gulls, terns, alcids, parids, fly-catchers, shrikes, and gnatcatchers are largely monochromatic, especially during the nonbreeding season. Sparrows tend to be various shades of brown. When colors are few or absent, look for conspicuous **markings** such as wing bars, eye rings, eye lines, breast streaks or spots, and tail spots. If you are looking at a flycatcher or a vireo, for example, the presence or absence of wing bars and eye rings is critical. If the bird in question is a sparrow, wing bars and breast markings are key.

With practice, you can learn to assess all of these traits—size, shapes, colors, and markings—in a matter of seconds. Remember, you are painting a mental picture in your mind's eye from which you will make your notes.

As important as what an unknown bird looks like is what it is doing. **Behavior** often simplifies bird identification. Is it eating seeds, fruits, or insects? Does it fly out from an exposed perch, catch a flying insect, then return to the same perch? If it swims, does it sit high or low in the water?

Does it dive? On land, does it run, walk, or hop? Is it nesting on the ground, in a bush, or in a cavity? In flight, does it hover, undulate, fly in a straight line, or soar on thermals? In trees, does it hitch its way up the trunk, run headfirst down the trunk, or spiral acrobatically around horizontal branches? By noting what the bird is doing and how it does it, your description becomes more complete.

Also listen to **sounds** the bird makes. They may be nonvocal or vocal. Woodpeckers drum on hollow branches. Mourning Doves' wings whistle in flight. Many bird songs can be described in words. Anyone can recognize "Old Sam Peabody, Peabody, Peabody" (White-throated Sparrow), "Zee, zee, zee, zoe, zee" (Black-throated Green Warbler), and "Who cooks for you? Who cooks for you-allll?" (Barred Owl).

Sometimes just the length of a song is conclusive. A few years ago, I spent some time on Hog Island, Maine, teaching an ornithology class at the National Audubon Society Ecology Camp. In the spruce-fir forest that dominates the island, I heard a loud, musically complex song. It seemed to go on forever. I timed several songs that lasted six or seven seconds. I could not find the singer, so when I got back to camp, I described the song to John Pumilio, a fellow instructor who has conducted several breeding bird censuses on the island. "Winter Wren," he said. "They nest here." The song's length was the key. Sure enough, when I found the bird the next day, it was a Winter Wren.

You can also compare bird vocalizations to other familiar sounds. A Bell's Vireo sounds like several smooth pebbles being rubbed vigorously between your hands. The Northern Parula's rising buzzy trill sounds like a fingernail being stroked along the teeth of a plastic comb. A Red-breasted Nuthatch sounds like a little tin horn. Even if you do not recognize a song or call, describe it. It may prove useful when using the field guide or describing the bird to a friend.

As long as an unfamiliar bird stays in view, study it and note size, shapes, colors, markings, behavior, and sounds. When the bird leaves, look around. Maybe you can find a distinctive nest. Oriole, vireo, hummingbird, phoebe, and swallow nests are easy to recognize. Such **ecological clues** are often helpful.

Describe the **habitat**. Savannah Sparrows are not likely to be seen in a forest, and Pileated Woodpeckers seldom frequent prairies.

Note your **geographical location**. Western Kingbirds seldom occur in Georgia, and Cerulean Warblers are unlikely in southern California.

Finally, record the **date**. Migrants appear at predictable times of the year. Most warblers, vireos, and tanagers head south for the winter and are unlikely to be seen in January, although there are exceptions. Yellow-rumped and Orange-crowned Warblers, for example, winter in some southern states. In the spring many of the finches and sparrows that keep temperate bird feeders busy all winter long head back to their northern breeding areas.

MAKING THE IDENTIFICATION

After studying an unknown bird as long as it permits and then recording all the pertinent details, you are ready to identify it. If you know your field guide intimately, flip to the most likely family group, such as shorebirds, owls, vireos, or sparrows, and compare your notes to the descriptions and plates. If your notes are complete, you will be able to identify most birds within a few minutes.

If you are not comfortable with your field guide, get to know it. Browse through it a few minutes each day until you can quickly page to each family. A field guide should be a help, not a hindrance.

If you are still searching for a good field guide, visit a library or bookstore and browse through those published by Houghton Mifflin (the Peterson guides), National Geographic, and Golden Press. I refer to them all from time to time, but I usually use National Geographic's *Field Guide to Birds of North America*. I prefer art to photos because an artist can illustrate every important field mark; photos reveal only those characteristics visible at the moment the shutter blinks. I also prefer having the range maps appear with the text and color plates. A collection of maps at the back of the book makes using it a bit less convenient.

Another powerful resource is computer-driven CD-ROM "field guides." Though impractical to take into the field, they are excellent tools for identifying birds from detailed notes. The combination of descriptive text, superior color graphics, range maps, and recordings of songs and calls makes CD-ROM technology the ultimate indoor bird-identification tool. If you do not have access to a computer, you can still compare the bird sounds you hear to recordings on cassettes and compact discs.

After identifying a new bird, it's a good idea to verify your conclusion. Call an experienced birder friend, describe the bird, answer any ensuing questions, then ask for his or her opinion. If you don't know any experienced birders, join the local Audubon Society or bird club and attend meetings. Members frequently compare notes on identification, and most enjoy helping others who may be stumped or just need confirmation.

You can access an entire network of experienced birders from all around the world by surfing the Internet. Most on-line services have birding forums where you can communicate with enthusiastic birders.

BINOCULARS AND SPOTTING SCOPES

Binoculars and spotting scopes bring distant birds up close so we can study them without intruding. Buy the best you can afford. Buy products that come with ten-year, twenty-year, or lifetime warranties. Be sure you can wear your binoculars for hours at a stretch without getting strained or tired. And be sure they focus to around 12 feet so you can take advantage of close encounters with warblers, vireos, and sparrows.

BACKYARD BIRDING BY EAR

"Drink your teeeeeee!"

"Witchity! Witchity! Witchity!"

"Teacher! TEACHER! TEACHER!"

These phrases resonate every spring across the wooded West Virginia ridge where I live. In fact, these songs, among many others, define the breeding season.

When I hear the first Rufous-sided Towhee's first invitation to tea in March, I know that apple blossoms cannot be far behind. When I hear the Common Yellowthroat's distinctive triplet, I know the warbler migration has begun. And when I hear the Ovenbird praise the educators of the world, I know most birds are on the nest.

Birding by ear is a lifelong challenge that comes easily to some, but more often, mastering this skill takes years of practice and experience. Many new bird-watchers consider it an impossible task. "It's all I can do to learn birds by sight," they say. "How can I possibly learn their songs, too?"

True, few can learn all the bird songs of North America, or even of a single state. But mastering the sounds of many backyard birds is relatively easy. The trick is going about it in the right way.

After learning to visually identify most of the birds that feed and nest in the backyard, it is only natural to learn to identify them by ear. Just as being able to identify birds by sight requires that you know what to look for, birding by ear requires knowing what to listen for. Some songs, such as the Indigo Bunting's and Black-headed Grosbeak's, are complex and difficult. Other birds, such as Eastern Phoebes and Whip-poor-wills, make it easy by singing their own names. Still others seem to speak English. The Barred Owl's "Who cooks for you, who cooks for you-allll?" is a classic example. The southern accent makes it all the more memorable.

No matter where you live, there are birds nearby that sing songs anyone can learn. Great Horned Owls, for example, live all across North America. They are the quintessential "hoot owl." They may be heard any time of year, but in many areas they kick off the breeding season in November or December. Their courtship includes a simple series of three to eight deep hoots.

Field guides often include a word description of birds' voices when appropriate, and I've learned to put words to bird songs to make them memorable. When I hear a Great Horned Owl, for example, I hear a hoot for each syllable in the phrase "Don't kill owls, save owls." There is nothing sacred about the specific words field guides or I attach to bird songs. Your ears may hear other words or sounds. That's perfectly all right. The point is to learn the technique of associating familiar words or sounds with birds' voices.

The familiar "caw" of the American Crow might be the most recognized bird sound in North America. American Kestrels, the small falcon most often seen perched on power lines and dead trees all across North America, communicate with a high-pitched "Killy, killy, killy." Killdeer, the most familiar and abundant member of the plover family, announce their presence each spring by shouting their own name: "Kill-dee! Kill-dee! Kill-dee!" The blood-curdling scream of a soaring Red-tailed Hawk often breaks the silence of a quiet morning walk. At dusk in spring and fall, Canada Geese honk their way to and from their nesting grounds. Wetlands resound with territorial male Red-winged Blackbirds singing "Kong-ka-reeee." And where you find Red-wings, also listen for the distinctive triplet of the Common Yellowthroat: "Witchity! Witchity, Witchity!"

Because of individual variation, not all members of a species sing exactly the same song. Yellowthroats, for example, sometimes sing a doubled-noted song: "Witchy! Witchy! Witchy!"

Other birds have regional dialects. Song Sparrows occur from coast to coast, but each of the subspecies sings a subtle variation of the basic Song Sparrow melody. The greater the geographical distance between subspecies, the greater the difference in their songs. Ornithologists use recordings and sonograms—graphic representations of song—to document this phenomenon. In some cases, subspecific variation is so obvious it can be detected by ear. If nothing else, these variations ensure that bird identification in all its various forms can take several lifetimes to master.

Another complicating factor is that some species have large repertoires of songs, whereas others sing just a basic song or two. Mockingbirds, catbirds, and thrashers sing dozens or even scores of songs on a daily basis. The champion North American singer is probably the Northern Mockingbird, for which more than 2,000 sounds have been recorded. Woodpeckers, swifts, and swallows, on the other hand, have limited vocal skills.

Not all vocalizations that birds make are songs. Some are calls. The difference between songs and calls can be confusing, but it is largely a difference of purpose. Birds (usually but not always males) sing to attract mates, to define the boundaries of territories, to defend territories, and to maintain the pair bond between male and female during the nesting season. Therefore, songs are usually associated with breeding activity. Birds call, on the other hand, to communicate the details of everyday life. An alarm call signals the presence of a predator. A rally call signals a brood of grouse chicks to assemble near the hen. Other calls maintain contact among members of a group, communicate the location of food, and signal agitation when social rules are violated.

Generally, songs are longer, louder, and more musical than calls. Their intent is to call attention to the singer. Calls tend to be brief, quieter, and less musical. Often they consist of a single note or two. The message is conveyed, but predators cannot zero in on such brief, soft sounds.

Despite the complication of intraspecific variation, many bird songs are easy to identify—sometimes too easy. On my first visit to Arizona in the mid-1970s, the morning chorus in the desert near Tucson was in full voice, and I heard a familiar cry: "Who cooks for you?" My field guide indicated that Barred Owls did not occur in southern Arizona, yet it sure sounded like a Barred Owl. However, the second phrase, "Who cooks for you-allll?" was missing. As I listened, I realized that many individuals were singing. A flock of Barred Owls in southern Arizona? Not likely. I listened more carefully and detected a dovelike quality to the sound, so I browsed through the species accounts in the field guide. Sure enough, White-winged Doves sing the first half of the Barred Owl song. It's a lesson I'll never forget.

Another of my favorite western birds, the Greater Pewee, occurs only in southeastern Arizona south into Mexico. It is sometimes called the Jose Maria bird because its song is a whistled "Ho-say, ma-re-ahhh."

Bell's Vireo inhabits the Great Plains and the extreme southwestern United States. Its song is distinctive not because it can be put into words, but rather because it sounds like something anyone can imitate. Take a handful of small, smooth pebbles and rub them vigorously between your two hands, as if trying to warm them in front of a fire. The sound you hear is a reasonable facsimile of a Bell's Vireo song.

Similarly, Brown-headed Nuthatches, which inhabit the pine forests of the Southeast, sound just like the double-noted squeak of a toy rubber duck. In northern coniferous forests, Red-breasted Nuthatches sound like little toy horns.

Sometimes it is only the songs of closely related species that allow us to tell them apart. The *Empidonax* flycatchers, all drab olive birds with wing bars, are a perfect example. So are the much more familiar Black-capped and Carolina Chickadees. Though there are subtle plumage differences, these two chickadees appear almost identical at first glance. Because their ranges largely do not overlap, geography is often the easiest way to separate this confusing pair. Along the border of their ranges, however, voice makes identification relatively simple. Black-caps whistle two clear, high-pitched notes: "Fee-bee." Carolina Chickadees, which live in my backyard, sing a similar song, but it typically has four notes: "Fee-bee, fee-bay." Once heard, the distinction is obvious.

There are dozens more examples of bird songs and calls that are easy to put into words or relate to familiar sounds. Learning bird songs is not nearly as difficult as most people think. They may all sound alike at first, but remember, they all looked alike at first, too.

To help you master bird songs, cassette tapes, compact discs, videotapes, and CD-ROMs of bird songs are available. Many such audio recordings are valuable encyclopedic references, but because they consist merely of a long series of bird names followed by songs and calls, they can be extremely tedious to use. One set of bird sounds that stands out above the rest is Houghton Mifflin's *Birding by Ear* series. Three volumes—east, west, and central—cover most North American species. What sets this series apart is its comprehensive scope and its instructional style. The narrator teaches the listener by arranging the species into groups of songs that are either similar or confusing. He then explains how each is unique and highlights the distinctive features of each song. If you are serious about learning bird songs, these are the recordings to use.

If you want to make learning bird songs as pleasant as possible, choose the CD format. On a CD you can access any song within seconds just by pressing a few buttons. Carrying a portable CD player into the field lets you check unfamiliar sounds almost instantly. Cassette tapes require a maddening amount of rewinding and fast-forwarding to locate individual species.

CD-ROM technology combines instant access of audio, video, and text references and is great for learning at a desk. Being able to see an image of a bird while it sings and read about its habits simultaneously is perhaps the most efficient way to learn birds by sight and sound. Birding videos are another option that combine sight and sound cues, but unless you enjoy sitting through the entire program, a lot of fast-forwarding and rewinding is required to customize your lesson.

The best way to learn bird songs is personally, from a mentor. I met Dr. Fred Baumgartner in Oklahoma in 1981 and had a chance to spend a half dozen weekends with him that spring. He, too, had learned from a master, Dr. Arthur Allen at Cornell University. Retired and in his seventies at the time, Dr. Baumgartner identified every song, call, and chip we heard. I never realized one man could know so much. I dogged him like a puppy and pummeled him with questions. He answered them all with patient encouragement. Learning bird songs has never come easily for me, and I continue to learn every year, but I'll be forever in Dr. Baumgartner's debt.

You may not know a professional ornithologist who can teach you bird songs, but local bird clubs, nature centers, and Audubon chapters sponsor bird walks throughout the year. Take advantage of these opportunities; let an experienced local birder be your mentor.

KEEPING RECORDS

FIELD NOTES

Birders observe, record, and analyze vast amounts of information. It is one of the most important things we do. Historically, paper and pens were any keen observer's primary tools. John James Audubon's journals and Arthur Cleveland Bent's classic life history series remind us of early ornithology's dependence on these simple tools.

Today, modern technology—computers, sophisticated optics, and audio and video recorders—allows both birders and professional ornithologists to process and organize vast amounts of information in ways that early ornithologists could not have even imagined. Field notes, regardless of how they are recorded, have been and will continue to be the backbone of ornithology.

For most it begins on a small scale. After a few years of enjoying birds at backyard feeders, you begin to realize the value of year-to-year comparisons. Maybe it's just a list on the refrigerator or notes on the calendar. Eventually, however, you buy a small notebook, and soon you find yourself taking notes on a weekly or even daily basis. Or perhaps you took a bird course at the local nature center and the instructor suggested that you record field notes.

Field notes are a permanent record of your observations. Treat them as such. Use permanent ink that won't smear when wet. It is, after all, a *field* notebook. Get in the habit of recording a standard set of information for each entry: date, time, weather conditions, and a detailed description of the location. Describe new or hard-to-find places in detail so that even a stranger could find it from your description.

A typical entry might read like this: "28 June 1973; 12:15 am; clear skies, about 75 degrees; Congo-Niantic Rd., top of Congo hill at Congo School, Montgomery Co., PA; coming home from work, saw a barn owl perched on telephone pole. It flew across road as I approached. Like a ghost, it disappeared into the blackness of the night."

This entry is significant for two reasons. First, I'd never seen a Barn Owl before, so the observation records a life bird. More important, however, is that Barn Owls have declined in abundance over the last twenty-five years. My notes serve as a record of a sighting.

Here are two other excerpts from my field notes. Both record important information and a very brief interpretation.

"2/23/84, west side of Lake Carl Blackwell, Payne County, OK. Mild, clear spring day. Box W-4 contains a dead, banded female bluebird. Apparently died during Dec/Feb cold snap. Band no. 1311-86584; banded as nestling 7/7/83 in box W-2. Suggests that at least some local resident bluebirds do not migrate. (Maybe they should.)"

"4/22/95. Fish Ridge, Marshall Co., WV. 10 am, cloudy, chilly. Large contingent of new birds arrived overnight. Saw/heard following this morning: wood thrush, scarlet tanager, white-eyed vireo, ovenbird, Louisiana waterthrush, parula, and black-and-white warblers. Blue-wing warblers arrived 3/19. First hummer showed up yesterday. Hummer on time, but warblers, WT, and ST seem early. Due to mild winter/spring here and south."

Field notes help me recall what I've seen in years past, and more importantly, they signal what I should look for in subsequent years. For example, here in northern West Virginia, I look for towhees and phoebes in early March, Chipping Sparrows in mid-April, hummers around April 22, and warblers the first week of May.

Keeping field notes also helps you become a better nature watcher. You learn to pay attention to detail. It fine-tunes your powers of observation. After you begin keeping field notes, you'll find yourself referring to them regularly. Where did you see your first Western Bluebird? Check your notes. When should you put up your hummingbird feeder? Check your notebook to see when hummers arrived the last few years.

Sometimes good field notes can have real social and ecological significance. A record of the way things are may be the best way to protect your favorite birding spots. When I lived in Oklahoma, a developer proposed building a mall in a bottomland forest floodplain. Members of the Payne County Audubon Society documented the ecological value of the area for flood control and wildlife by gathering notes and photographs that had been compiled by local residents over the years. We presented our case to the city commission, and it denied the developers the permits they needed to use the site.

You need not be a skilled writer to keep field notes. You are mainly doing this for yourself, so keep the notes brief and informal. Write in phrases. Abbreviate, but be clear enough so that others might someday understand your message. Don't worry about grammar or spelling. The only inviolate rule is to keep it legible so you can read it in the future.

If you cannot afford a camera, illustrate your notes with drawings. Even stick figures with arrows pointing to key features can help a more knowledgeable birder identify an unknown bird. Nests, eggs, and landmarks might also be easier to draw than to describe in words. No one will grade your notebook, and neatness does not count, although both your note-taking and drawing skills will improve with experience.

Record both the facts and your interpretation of them. In retrospect, I enjoy my feelings about an event as much as the event itself. I'll always remember that first hammering Pileated Woodpecker, singing Whip-poor-will, booming prairie chicken, and dancing woodcock.

Trips to distant places are especially noteworthy. In 1983 I saw my first Elegant Trogon near Portal, Arizona. In 1987, after ten previous trips to Mexico, I saw Stygian Owls and Chestnut-sided Shrike-Vireos. In Ecuador in 1995 I saw Club-winged Manakins displaying on the lek and a Sword-billed Hummingbird perched quietly on a branch just above a trail.

Less exotic locations can be equally exciting. Trips to Alaska, southeastern Arizona, the Texas coast, the Florida Everglades, Pennsylvania's Hawk Mountain, and Cape May, New Jersey guarantee pages of notebook fodder. Even my own backyard seldom fails to yield at least one notable event anytime I sally forth.

For those who resist the idea of note taking, printed lists of local and state birds are available at nature centers and state conservation departments. The American Birding Association (P.O. Box 6599, Colorado Springs, CO 80934) publishes the *ABA Checklist: Birds of the Continental United States and Canada*. At the very least, such lists allow birders to record first sightings of life birds.

USING THE COMPUTER

Personal computers that help organize our lives can also help organize our birding activities. Database managers allow anyone to create useful systems for storing field notes. They can be organized by date, place, and species and can be used to compare year-to-year observations almost instantaneously.

If setting up your own database system seems beyond your ability, many birding software packages are on the market. The most sophisticated include range maps and interactive help for identifying birds by both sight and sound. The most useful for recording and analyzing daily observations are computerized world and country checklists. These eliminate the tedium of typing in bird names and allow you to concentrate on the key information: time, place, conditions, and observations. If you are more concerned with state, county, or even backyard lists, many programs allow you to create your own customized lists.

Birding software is not cheap, so study what is available and be sure the program you buy does what you expect it to. Also beware of the costs associated with upgrading outdated programs, and be sure upgrades do not require you to reenter your observations.

Computers also provide birders with ready access to one another via the "information superhighway." Communication services such as America Online enable anyone with a computer and a modem to meet and share information electronically. It's a great way to compare notes and meet people interested in just about every facet of birding.

USING PHOTOGRAPHIC EQUIPMENT

Photographic equipment is an important tool for recording field observations. From the comfort of your living room, a 35mm camera with a telephoto lens allows you to supplement written notes with photographs of backyard observations. If a rare or unknown bird shows up at your feeder, document it with a photograph. When trying to identify an unknown bird, a picture truly is worth a thousand words. When you find a nest, photograph the eggs and nest, and then step back and take a long shot of the habitat. Now you have a visual record of the bird's nesting habitat. (When shooting nests, do not permanently alter the habitat, and beware that you might leave a scent trail that predators might follow.)

Get in the habit of keeping the camera handy at home and in the car, and you might capture an award-winning or sellable image. How often have you seen something from the house or car that you wish you could have recorded on film?

Video cameras offer birders a chance to make their own nature documentaries. Record the birds on the feeder to make an identification guide for the local bird club. When you review the tape, you can focus on such things as the subtle differences between Downy and Hairy Woodpeckers.

Away from the house, you can use your car as a blind. Set up 30 feet from a nest box, and record the comings and goings of a pair of bluebirds or chickadees after the eggs hatch. During that first week after hatching, parents bring food to the nest at two- to five-minute intervals. With continuing video footage, you can measure the rate at which parents feed their young and document what the nestlings are being fed. If you have the time and patience, venture into the woods and record a strutting turkey, drumming grouse, or singing warbler. Best of all, with a video record, you can review the event repeatedly and discover what can be missed in a blink of an eye.

A photographic record is especially helpful for recording the status of various habitats and natural areas. A photograph or video of a favorite place might prove invaluable when a conservation group tries to protect the area ten years later.

USING AUDIO RECORDERS

Another helpful device is a cassette tape recorder. Many people prefer to record their notes on tape and transfer them later to a permanent notebook. This technique allows you to record a lot of detailed information quickly and accurately, but beware—mechanical devices are prone to failure. Always carry extra batteries, and always carry a backup notebook and pen—just in case.

Audio recorders can also be used to record unfamiliar bird calls and songs. Rather than try to describe a new sound on paper, record it. Parabolic microphones, used by ornithologists to record bird sounds in the field, are readily available to serious birders. You can take the tape of the unknown bird home and compare the recording to sounds on reference tapes and CDs.

APPENDIX A

SHADE COFFEE

From the courtyard of the hacienda near the tiny village of San Antonio in the southwestern Mexican state of Colima, we set out on foot. One group headed back the paved road toward Comala; the other ambled along a rutted rocky road toward the Laguna El Jabali. By midmorning, my two groups of eager birders had compiled an impressive list of mountain birds. The most spectacular resident species included Mountain Trogons, Masked Tityras, Tufted Flycatchers, Stripe-backed and Red-headed Tanagers, Ivory-billed Woodcreepers, Happy Wrens, Berylline Hummingbirds, and West Mexican Chachalacas. To that list of residents, we added more than a dozen species of Neotropical warblers more commonly seen north of the border. They were winter visitors just like us.

Given the montane setting and the mature forest just beyond the edge of the road, none of these birds came as a surprise. What did surprise me was that the entire area was an active coffee plantation. I didn't expect such terrific birding in the midst of a working farm. The first time I visited San Antonio back in the mid-1980s, I learned firsthand that coffee is a shrub that grows best in the shade of a mature forest canopy. Traditionally, coffee has been grown on forested plantations as a shade-loving crop. Consequently, coffee production and bird conservation complemented each other.

"Our studies in the Dominican Republic show that there's no difference between levels of bird survival in shaded coffee plantations and native forests," explains Joseph Wunderle of the International Institute of Tropical Forestry.

It seemed the best of both worlds. Forest birds thrived in the canopy; coffee thrived below. Ecological, economic, and agricultural interests converged in harmony. It seemed too good to be true. It was.

Unbeknownst to me, the dream had begun to unravel into an ecological nightmare in the late 1970s. Major coffee producers discovered that by removing the canopy, coffee grew faster and produced higher yields. Unfortunately, the cost for "sun" coffee's higher productivity, beyond the ecological devastation that accompanied the destruction of the canopy, included expensive fertilizers and pesticides. The switch to sun coffee also led to serious erosion where coffee plantations occupied rugged terrain.

Over the last twenty years, sun coffee has come to dominate the market. Many large coffee growers have switched to new coffee hybrids that produce more beans under full sun. They favor short-term gains and ignore the long-term ecological tolls such as loss of critical habitat for forest birds and dependence upon expensive agri-chemicals. Large coffee plantations led the way because they could afford the expense required to grow sun coffee. Small family growers languished in a shrinking market.

The impact of converting to sun coffee plantations has been ornithologically disastrous. According to a fact sheet published by the Smithsonian Migratory Bird Center, field studies in Mexico and Colombia have found 94 to 97 percent fewer bird species in sun-grown coffee plantations than on shade-grown coffee farms. Furthermore, the amount of land planted in coffee under reduced shade conditions ranges from 17 percent in Mexico to 40 percent in Costa Rica and 69 percent in Colombia.

In recent years, however, entrepreneurs, birders, and small coffee growers formed an enterprising alliance to create both a supply and a demand for bird-friendly, shade-grown coffee. They realize that preserving the forest canopy saves birds.

According to Greg Butcher, former executive director of the American Birding Association (ABA) and now editor of *Birder's World* magazine, "There are 60 million bird-watchers in the U.S. If we all demand shade-grown coffee, we can help conserve family farms that—as far as birds are concerned—are forests. We believe birders can make a powerful impact on the way coffee is grown. . . and that shade-grown coffee can help restore migratory songbird habitat in Central America."

The ABA feels so strongly about shade coffee that it has entered into a cooperative program with the California-based Thanksgiving Coffee Company. Paul Katzeff, CEO of Thanksgiving Coffee, was among the first in the coffee business to recognize an unusual opportunity to mix birds and business. In June 1997, Thanksgiving introduced Songbird Coffees, six blends of bird-friendly shade-grown java.

The results exceeded Katzeff's wildest dreams. "Songbird Coffee," he reports, "is the most successful new product introduction I've seen in twenty-five years." In just the last half of 1997, Thanksgiving Coffee sold more than

80,000 packages of Songbird Coffees. And for each pound of Songbird Coffee sold, Thanksgiving Coffee Company returns 15 cents to the ABA to support conservation programs. That translated to $12,000 for the ABA in just the first eight months that Songbird Coffees were on the market.

At first, Songbird Coffees were sold only in Wild Birds Unlimited and Wild Oats stores across the country. Slowly, however, Songbird Coffees have begun appearing on shelves in independent bird stores and garden centers. And Butcher suggests that a huge untapped market are the "in-house" coffee pots at businesses all across the country. It might begin at the editorial offices of bird magazines and conservation organizations, but those 60 million birders could soon have shade coffee brewing in offices and boardrooms everywhere.

Eventually, as understanding of and demand for environmentally friendly brews spill over from the birding public to all who enjoy and appreciate ecological diversity, shade coffees might even appear on the shelves of traditional supermarkets.

Another major player in the shade coffee story is Fred Houk of Counter Culture Coffee in Durham, North Carolina. Counter Culture markets a family of shade coffees under the Sanctuary label. Counter Culture also prepares a shade coffee for the Wild Bird Centers of America stores called Canopy Coffee.

Wild Bird Center COO Jane Crowley says, "We launched our Canopy Coffees in September 1997, and they are doing very well. And two of our products were rated first and second in a taste test by *Coffee Review Magazine*."

A small percentage of the price of both Sanctuary and Canopy Coffees goes to the National Fish and Wildlife Foundation, a private nonprofit conservation group. The NFWF matches each contribution and uses the fund to help Latin American coffee growers improve bird conservation on their properties.

For shade coffee to succeed commercially, however, coffee-drinking birders must be willing to change their buying habits and pay a bit more. They seem more than willing to do both.

The premium price consumers pay for eco-friendly coffee is modest. "We can save a lot of forested family farms if people are willing to pay just one penny more per cup," says Daniel Katz, executive director of the Rainfall Alliance, an organization pioneering efforts to certify tropical products from eco-friendly sources. "The premium price will give farmers the incentive to stay green, and it will help ensure the survival of some of the earth's most cherished birds and wildlife."

Price controls every commodity. If consumers are willing to pay more for a bird-friendly brew, coffee farmers will grow it. By creating a demand, consumers can manipulate the coffee market to once again favor birds.

No matter how environmentally friendly shade coffee may be, though, if it doesn't taste good, no one will buy it. At the Birdwatch America trade show in Atlanta one year, I skulked around Thanksgiving Coffee's booth. Staff provided samples to everyone who stopped by, and most were eager to taste the new brew. Over the course of about an hour, I eavesdropped on more than twenty-five conversations. I didn't hear a single bad review, and more than half remarked that the Songbird blend tasted better than their store-bought coffees, which were almost certainly sun coffees. The most impressive testimonial regarding the taste of shade coffee comes from Thanksgiving CEO Katzeff: "Of the first 80,000 packages of Songbird Coffees we sold," he said, "not a single one came back because a customer was dissatisfied or didn't like the coffee. We got a few returns on defective or torn bags, but not a single complaint about the product itself."

Furthermore, Katz hopes other members of the birding industry will use the success of shade coffee as an environmental/economic model for manufacturing other bird-related products. I've already seen wooden bird feeders and nest boxes that specify that no old-growth timber has been used to make the product. Could organically grown birdseed find a market? Katzeff thinks so.

Thanksgiving's commitment to shade coffee seems to have been worth the risk of paying 40 to 70 percent above market rate for organically grown shade coffee. They keep the total cost down by buying directly from growers and eliminating middlemen. They get to know their growers, visit their farms, and meet their families. Their goal is to create a demand for shade coffee that will stop the destruction of forests and even force reforestation in countries that want to maintain coffee as a major cash crop.

But how can consumers be sure that shade coffee is truly shade grown? The Rainforest Alliance is an organization pioneering the use of labels to certify tropical products from eco-friendly sources. To earn an ECO-OK label, a farming operation must protect trees, soils, water, workers, and local residents.

The criteria to earn the ECO-OK seal of approval are strict—tough enough to protect workers and the environment, but practical enough to be met with existing technology and knowledge. In reality, there is not yet a universally accepted certification program for shade coffee. Roasters and retailers prefer to rely on their own reputations and credibility. As long as the shade coffee business continues to grow and contributions continue to be made to bird conservation programs, a universal certification program is unlikely to catch on.

Though shade coffee may not yet be available at supermarkets, don't underestimate the power consumers hold. Contact the manager of your grocery store, and write to coffee makers. Explain the benefits of shade coffee, and ask them to offer it. Explain that helping migratory and tropical birds is worth a few extra pennies per cup. Until shade coffee is available at the neighborhood grocery, take your coffee dollars elsewhere. Shade coffee is good for birds, birders, coffee growers, and coffee packagers.

For decades, conservationists have struggled to prove to cash-strapped Latin American farmers that conserving tropical forests is in their best economic interests. The success of shade coffee stands as a shining example.

APPENDIX B

FURTHER INFORMATION

To learn more about backyard birds and other wildlife, contact the following nonprofit organizations. Membership in each organization provides a variety of benefits such as magazine subscriptions, discounted admission fees, and invitations to participate in special events.

American Bird Conservancy
1250 24th St. NW, Suite 400
Washington, DC 20037

American Birding Association
P.O. Box 6599
Colorado Springs, CO 80934

Bat Conservation International
P.O. Box 162603
Austin, TX 78716

Cape May Bird Observatory
701 E. Lake Drive
Cape May Point, NJ 08212

Cornell Lab of Ornithology
(Home of Project FeederWatch and Nest Box Network)
159 Sapsucker Woods Road
Ithaca, NY 14850

Hawk Mountain Sanctuary Association
1700 Hawk Mountain Road
Kempton, PA 19529-9449

Ladybird Johnson Wildflower Center
4801 LaCrosse Ave.
Austin, TX 78739

National Audubon Society
700 Broadway
New York, NY 10003

National Bird-Feeding Society
P.O. Box 23
Northbrook, IL 60065

National Wildlife Federation
8925 Leesburg Pike
Vienna, VA 22184

North American Bluebird Society
P.O. Box 74
Darlington, WI 53530

North American Butterfly Association
909 Birch Street
Baraboo, WI 53913

Purple Martin Conservation Association
Edinboro University of Pennsylvania
Edinboro, PA 16444

REFERENCE BOOKS

A few reference books you might find useful include *Bird Watcher's Digest* Special Publication Series, which includes books on nest boxes, bluebirds, martins, bats, butterflies, wildflowers, and hummingbirds; Stackpole Books' Wild Bird Guides, which include *American Goldfinch, Black-capped Chickadee, Northern Cardinal, Tufted Titmouse, Downy Woodpecker, Red-tailed Hawk,* and more; special publications from the Minnesota Department of Natural Resources, including *Wild About Birds: The DNR Feeding Guide, Woodworking for Wildlife: Homes for Birds and Mammals,* and *Landscaping for Wildlife,* all by Carroll Henderson.